Multidimensional
Terrorism

Multidimensional Terrorism

edited by
Martin Slann &
Bernard Schechterman

Lynne Rienner Publishers, Inc. • Boulder & London

Published in the United States of America in 1987 by
Lynne Rienner Publishers, Inc.
948 North Street, Boulder, Colorado 80302

Library of Congress Cataloging-in-Publication Data

Multidimensional terrorism.

  Bibliography: p.
  Includes index.
  1. Terrorism.   2. Terrorism—Case studies.
I. Slann, Martin W.   II. Schechterman, Bernard B.
HV6431.M84   1987   303.6'25   87-4898
ISBN 1-55587-030-9 (lib. bdg.)

Printed and bound in the United States of America

The paper used in this publication meets the
requirements of the American National Standard
for Permanence of Paper for Printed Library
Materials Z39.48-1984 ∞

To our parents, wives, and children

Contents

Tables and Figures

Tables

Figures

Introduction

MARTIN SLANN

Although terrorism is an ancient political curse, its various motivations and dimensions are only now being explored in some detail. This volume pursues explanations of aspects of terrorism by highlighting and examining several basic theoretical approaches to the subject and offering complementary case studies.

Part of the difficulty in either fully analyzing or understanding political terrorism has to do with the fact that there is a myriad of terrorist organizations and terrorist agendas. Many of these organizations have remarkable longevity, while others commit a single horrendous act and disappear or undergo a name change. Several are state supported, and some are in fact appendages of a terrorist state's foreign policy. Also, there are individuals who, while not terrorists—because they do not yet perceive themselves to be threatened with physical extermination—are willing to do whatever they think is necessary to ensure their survival. Consider, for example, the view of a determined Israeli who believes that nothing is forbidden when it comes to survival:

> Me, I don't mind being a Qaddafi. I'm not looking to the gentiles for admiration and I don't need their love. But I don't need it from your kind of Jew, either. I want to survive. And my intention happens to be that my children will survive, too. With or without the blessing of the Pope or assorted Torah sages from the New York *Times*. If anyone raises a hand against my children, I'll destroy him—and his children— with or without your vaunted 'purity of arms.' And I don't give a damn if he's a Christian or a Moslem or a Jew or a pagan. Throughout history, anyone who thought he was above killing got killed. It's an iron-clad rule.[1]

Such a point of view is reminiscent of a Hobbesian state of nature. However, it is also indicative of a certain rationale of violence. Terrorists, after all, maintain that they are abandoning the more humane norms of society because they were first abandoned by those who give lip-service to these norms. Victims of injustice tend to appeal to a higher morality.

Grant Wardlaw has observed that, "at base, terrorism is a moral problem."[2] Terrorists, in most instances, view themselves as moral agents. Their activities and goals are motivated within a dimension of absolutism; their cause is all-important and all-consuming. For terrorists there is no morally neutral ground, and therefore there cannot be anyone who is blameless. It is more than simply a case of the stark choice of being either for or against. If an individual is not an advocate of the righteous cause (a "true believer"),[3] then he or she is guilty of the sin of omission.

However terrorism is examined, then, and whether it assumes the dimension of state, individual, or group terrorism, it is important to note that there is usually a dramatic element of the self-righteous. The brutal acts of terrorists are not motivated by those who are unsure of the worthiness of their cause. The fact that many terrorists and (perhaps especially) terrorist governments operate under the inspiration of a moral imperative is instructive. In this sense the terrorist is provincial: assuming the perfect reasonableness and justice of the cause, it is irrational and unjust to oppose or ignore the cause.

Self-righteousness is both a characteristic and a rationale for those who carry out acts of terrorism. This is a messianic quality that many terrorists, regardless of their ideological persuasion, generally share.[4] For most terrorists there can be no compromise with evil. The enemy and his accomplices in desecration must be completely destroyed.

Terrorists see themselves as having been coerced into using violence as a political tool because violence is the only tool that remains to be used. No other political recourse has worked. Therefore, the violence committed by a terrorist is not necessarily caused by him.[5]

Evidence that terrorists consider themselves to be innocent victims of a provocative political establishment can be seen in terrorist rhetoric.[6] For example, combatting the "terror of the ruling class"[7] was the professed aim of one Italian terrorist organization. (In a real way such an aim is reminiscent of the "terror of virtue" of the French Revolution.[8]) Terrorism is seen in this context as being visited upon those who are so guilty of political sin that they get what they richly deserve. For instance, in explaining how a Christian physician can become one of the most notorious organizers of terrorism in the Middle East, George Habash stated in a 1970 interview that he blames his violence on the Israelis.

> They forced us to flee. It is a picture that haunts me and that I'll never forget. Thirty thousand human beings walking, weeping . . . screaming in terror . . . women with babies in their arms and children tugging at their skirts . . . and the Israeli soldiers pushing them on with guns. Some people fell by the wayside, some never got up again. It was terrible. One thinks: this isn't life, this isn't human. Once you have seen this, your heart and your brain are transformed. . . . What's the point of healing a sick body when such things can happen? One must change the world, do something, kill if necessary, kill even at the risk of becoming inhuman in our turn.[9]

It needs to be mentioned that in the midst of what appears to be irrational violence there can be found both a reason and a rationale: "The magic of terrorism has always been its power of magnification: an act of violence which would be too puny to be noticed if it were directed against the armed forces of a state can be turned into a psychological blow strong enough to shake a society if it is directed against a few ordinary and innocent people."[10] The victims of terrorists should not take the attacks personally. The attacks are political statements intended to intimidate and persuade. The question "Why me?" is irrelevant. No one is innocent, and everyone is expendable.

In this book, we have tried to cover the basic aspects of terrorism, with both theoretical pieces and case studies. To clarify the more evident dimensions of terrorism, Norman Provizer begins Part 1 with an essay on the difficulties of definition. Also in Part 1 are chapters on "rational" and "irrational" terrorism, authored respectively by Robert Maranto and Bernard Schechterman. These pieces focus on the goals and motivations of terrorists, as well as on the disconcerting evidence that even the irrational can have its own rationales.

In Part 2, several relevant (and often overlooked) dimensions of terrorism are considered. Richard Leeman addresses the rhetoric of terrorism in order to explain how it is that "terrorism is a futile endeavor, yet it is on the rise." Martin Slann writes on the most effective and durable dimension of terrorism, the state. Joseph R. Goldman analyzes the variant threats a democratic society faces from terrorism, noting that there must be preparations to confront terrorism on several possible fronts, including the nuclear one.

Several case studies are provided in Part 3 in order to illustrate the dimensions identified in the earlier sections. Leonard Weinberg and William Eubank discuss the motivations, including family relationships, of Italian terrorists. Violent modes of behavior have been exemplified by the revolutionary regime in Iran since 1979; as Gregory Rose demonstrates, collective action can be a most effective means of unifying a population under a government that is an active sponsor of violent activities. Michael Gunter in "Turkey and the Armenians," suggests how governments may protect themselves or, in the case of Turkey, opt for severe counterterrorism as a means of applying security strategies. Edward P. Moxon-Browne's essay on Northern Ireland touches on the most evident cause of terrorism: political and social alienation can lead to and even justify the kind of desperate atmosphere that furnishes ample reason for terrorism. Finally, William Lasser discusses the problems that free societies face in seeking to combat terrorism without destroying democracy itself.

Notes

[1.] Amos Oz, *In The Land of Israel* (New York: Vintage Books, 1984), p. 87.

[2.] Grant Wardlaw, *Political Terrorism* (Cambridge: Cambridge University Press, 1982), p. 4.

[3.] See, of course, the classic work by Eric Hoffer, *The True Believer* (New York: Harper & Row, 1951).

[4.] One other quality terrorists share is their concomitant need for money, often for nonviolent purposes. Not all terrorists are simply fanatical. The Palestine Liberation Organization is an example of a movement that maintains health clinics as well as commits terrorist acts. See *The Wall Street Journal*, 21 July 1986, pp. 1 and 11. How terrorist groups are financed is not covered in this volume, but it is a dimension of terrorism in need of examination. It is expensive to be violent.

[5.] Not that violence cannot be used as a first resort. The Assassins during the twelfth and thirteenth centuries were determined to reach immediate paradise via martyrdom. They viewed their victims as obstinate enemies of Islam whom they were morally obligated to murder.

[6.] See Richard Leeman, "Rhetoric and Values in Terrorism," Chapter 6 in this volume.

[7.] *Ibid.*

[8.] Oriana Fallaci, "A Leader of the Fedeyeen: 'We Want a War Like the Vietnam War,'" *Life*, 12 June 1970, p. 34.

[9.] *The Economist*, 26 July 1986, p. 9. This gives credence to the ancient Chinese saying, "Kill one, frighten ten thousand."

[10.] *Ibid.*

Part 1

Theory Building and Terrorism

Defining Terrorism

1

NORMAN W. PROVIZER

"We live," to borrow the words of J. Bowyer Bell, "in a time of terror."[1] Whatever debates exist over the exact scope and salience of this phenomenon, the emergence of terrorism as a major issue in the contemporary world remains an incontrovertible fact of political life. As *Sunday Times* defence correspondent Tony Geraghty noted in his introduction to the Royal United Services Institute for Defence Studies survey *Ten Years of Terrorism* (published in 1979), "Over the last ten years, terrorism in Europe has moved out of the fictitious world of James Bond to become a contemporary problem as ubiquitous as drug abuse and environmental pollution."[2]

Of course, neither the term nor the phenomenon it attempts to reflect is new to the world. Some 900 years ago, the "Society of Assassins," founded by Hassan Ibn Sabah, used the weapon of assassination as a tool of terror: a tool that made the Society "...a powerful force in the Arab world for 200 years...."[3] And, with the French Revolution and the Reign of Terror, the term clearly gained its foothold in history.[4]

Yet the explosion in interest in terrorism qua terrorism is of much more recent vintage. This point is brought home by an examination of the entries in two major, annotated, bibliographic volumes on the subject - one compiled by Norton and Greenberg, the other by Edward Mickolus.[5] In both cases, somewhere between 99.6 and 99.7 percent of the general works cited were published from 1968 on. Little wonder then that Bowyer Bell and others address contemporary history in epochal terms regarding the phenomenon of terrorism.

The attention given terrorism, however, has not been without its frustrations: the primary one of which is the seeming inability to define the term in a universally accepted fashion. Bowyer Bell could label the modern era as "a time of terror," while also arguing "...there is no satisfactory political definition of terror extant or forthcoming, there is similarly no common academic consensus as to the essence of terror and no common language with which to shape a model acceptable to political scientists or social psychologists."[6] "No one," in other words, "has a definition of terrorism."[7] Though the subject has moved out of the shadows onto the center stage of global interest, it continues to lead a penumbra-like existence, definitionally speaking.

To understand terrorism, "one must seek to understand what is happening to whom, where, when, how, why and with what outcomes and effects."[8] There has been no shortage of efforts to link such factors together in definitional packages, only a shortage of agreement as to value of the packages produced. As such, it is not that "no one" possesses a definition of terrorism, but that everyone has his or her own definition of the

3

phenomenon.

This problem is well illustrated in the single, most comprehensive, published survey on terrorism - the volume *Political Terrorism: A Research Guide to Concepts, Theories, Data Bases and Literature* by Alex Schmid.[9] In a questionnaire distributed to authors in the field, Schmid, of the Centre For the Study of Social Conflicts at the State University of Leiden in the Netherlands, asked, "Whose definition of terrorism do you find adequate for your purposes?" The highest number of citations went to "no adequate definition" (10), followed by the "my own definition is adequate" response (9). Five definitions were cited by more than one respondent in the survey. E.V. Walter was on the top of this list with five citations. Thomas Thornton, Martha Crenshaw (Hutchinson), Paul Wilkinson, and Brian Jenkins (with Janera Johnson) each had three citations. The United States Advisory Committee on Criminal Justice was cited twice and 22 other sources were cited once by the survey's respondents.[10]

The same questionnaire also asked the participants in the select sample how they felt about efforts to reach commonly accepted definitions "in the field of political violence in general and terrorism in particular." Here, 56 percent of the 50 respondents expressed the view that such agreement was a "necessary precondition for cumulative research."[11]

When the lack of definitional consensus is combined with the perceived need for such consensus in the study of terrorism, the student of the subject appears to face an intractable barrier. Yet that is not quite the case. Though definitional disagreements are abundant, there is, nevertheless, a common image of terrorist activities: an image sufficiently clear to allow data gathering to take place and the data bases produced to gain wide recognition. The Rand Corporation Chronology of International Terrorism and the ITERATE Project (International Terrorism: Attributes of Terrorist Events) available through the Inter-University Consortium for Political and Social Research in Ann Arbor represent two such efforts.[12]

In the Rand Chronology, international terrorism is *described* as "...a single incident or a campaign of violence waged outside the presently accepted rules and procedures of international diplomacy and war. It is often designed to attract worldwide attention to the existence and cause of the terrorists and to inspire fear. Often the violence is carried out for effect. The actual victim or victims of terrorist attacks and the target audience may not be the same; the victims may be totally unrelated to the struggle."[13]

For the ITERATE Project, terrorism was operationally defined as "...the use, or threat of use, of anxiety-inducing extra-normal violence for political purpose by any individual or group, whether acting for or in opposition to established governmental authority, when such action is intended to influence the attitudes and behavior of a target group wider than the immediate victims and when, through the nationality or foreign ties of its perpetrators, its location, the nature of its institutional or human victims or the mechanics of its resolution, its ramifications transcend national boundaries." Under ITERATE, international terrorism involves such activity wherein the perpetrators are controlled by states, while in transnational terrorism the perpetrators are essentially autonomous non-state actors.[14]

Neither the Rand description nor the ITERATE operational definition is without flaws. Still, they have been sufficient to offer reasonable working approaches to data gathering. The reason for this is that despite differing definitions of terrorism, there remains a certain sense of congruence concerning many of the critical elements associated with the phenomenon.

Based on a content analysis of 109 definitions of terrorism, Schmid describes the frequency with which certain elements appear.[15] First on the frequency chart is the element of violence/force at 83.5 percent, followed by political intent at 65 percent. An emphasis on fear/terror is the third-ranking element found in over half of the definitions in the sample (51 percent).

The ideas of threat and psychological effects and anticipated reactions are next on the list (at 47 and 41.5 percent respectively). The distinction drawn between the victims and the actual targets of terrorism represents the sixth-ranked element (at 37.5 percent), while purposive/systematically planned action stands as the seventh-ranked element (at 32 percent). Discussions of the actual method of combat/strategy/tactics, the lack of humanitarian constraints linked to the violation of accepted norms of behavior, and the use of coercion/extortion to induce compliance round out the top ten elements in the frequency chart (at 30.5, 30 and 28 percent respectively).

Two added elements - publicity and the act's impersonal/indiscriminate character - appear with frequencies over 20 percent (21.5 and 21 percent). Six more elements fall within the more-than-10-but-less-than-20 percent frequency range. They are: emphasis on the civilian/noncombatant status of victims (17.5 percent); emphasis on intimidation (17 percent); emphasis on the innocence of the victims (15.5 percent); emphasis on a group/movement as perpetrator (14 percent); and emphasis on the act's symbolic/demonstrational dimension (13.5 percent).

The 22 elements in the Schmid frequency chart end with the unpredictability of the act (9 percent), its clandestine nature (9 percent), its repetitive aspect (7 percent), its criminal nature (6 percent) and the demands it places on third parties (4 percent).

Such a checklist does not provide a definition per se. In fact, Schmid notes that the exercise in analyzing the frequency distribution of the elements of terrorism does not lead to "... a true or correct definition of terrorism."[16] But if a definition providing for consistent use of the term by all parties remains a chimera, the frequency analysis does point to the central elements connected to terrorism upon which considerable agreement exists.

This agreement provides the basis, then, for Schmid's attempt at definition:

> Terrorism is a method of combat in which random
> or symbolic victims serve as instrumental *target(s) of*
> *violence.* These instrumental victims share group or

5

class characteristics which form the basis for their selec-
tion for victimization. Through previous use of violence
or the credible threat of violence other members of that
group or class are put in a *state of chronic fear (terror)*.
This group or class, whose members' sense of security is
purposively undermined, is the *target of terror*. The victimization of the target of violence is considered ex-
tranormal by most observers from the witnessing audience on the basis of its atrocity; the time (e.g.
peacetime) or place (not a battlefield) of victimization
or the disregard for rules of combat accepted in conventional warfare. The norm violation creates an attentive
audience beyond the target of terror; sectors of this audience might in turn form the main object of manipula-
tion. The purpose of this indirect method of combat is
either to immobilize the target of terror in order to produce disorientation and/or compliance, or to mobilize
secondary *targets of demands* (e.g. a government) or
targets of attention (e.g. public opinion) to changes of
attitude or behavior favoring the short or long-term interests of the users of this method of combat.[17]

Schmid's definitional effort gives considerable attention to the target
dimension of terrorism (distinguishing victims of violence not only from the
actual target of terror but also from targets of demand and attention).[18] It
further focuses on the dimensions of purpose and context, and, to a lesser
extent, on the acts that differentiate terrorism from other violent activities.
Schmid's approach, however, consciously avoids dealing with motives - a
dimension that is often used to separate crusaders from criminals or crazies,
and, as such, one that is closely related to the second-ranked citation in his
frequency chart, i.e., political intent.[19] This definitional effort also says little about the perpetrators of terrorism, thereby implying that there is no
unique attribute of the phenomenon linked to those who carry it out. In this
sense, it sidesteps the extremely contentious debate over whether direct or
indirect terror used as state policy is indistinguishable from the insurgency
or challenge terrorism that has captured international headlines and attention.[20] Similarly, the elimination of a description of perpetrators from the
"definition" turns distinctions drawn between transnational terrorism and
other manifestations of terror-using and inducing activities into what is, at
best, a secondary consideration.

Though there is significant support for the expansive view of terrorism,
which blurs such lines under the call for academic objectivity, there are also
serious questions about the ultimate utility and value of the expansive approach.[21] Take, for example, Schmid's discussion of the Reign of Terror. In
his words, "Those who had originally supported the draconian measures of
Robespierre began to fear for their lives and conspired to overthrow him.
They could not accuse him of the Terror since they had declared it to be the

legitimate form of government, so they accused him of 'Terrorism' which had an illegal and repulsive flavour.''[22]

In this context, the switch appears to be nothing more than a game of political semantics in which a negative label is substituted for a positive one. Yet there is more to it than that. The state variable carries with it important implications that should not be readily dismissed. From a judgmental perspective, this does not mean that "thugs" who hold office are somehow better than "thugs" without state positions who wantonly slaughter innocents. The excessive and difficult to justify violence of state terror is neither more nor less moral than anti-state terrorism. But the shared component of "terror" does not mean that it is profitable, in either intellectual or policy terms, to collapse two distinct phenomena into a single category. The boundary maintenance problems involved in the concept of terrorism are severe enough without this type of overextension. Look, for example, at the question of nuclear weapons. In the future, if terrorists of the transnational kind were to gain access to nuclear weapons, would one then argue that such a situation is indistinguishable from the nuclear "balance of terror" that came into existence soon after the end of World War II? Or, quite to the contrary, would one examine common elements while still recognizing the differing conditions that distinguish the two phenomena?

It seems rather obvious that the latter, conceptually narrower path makes considerably more sense than the path of overextension. After all, as Louis René Beres notes in his discussion of a nuclear apocalypse, "...terrorist groups tend to operate under a different meaning of rationality than do states...terrorists are often insensitive to the kinds of retaliatory threats that are the traditional mainstay of order between states."[23] In short, the state variable matters.

Essentially, terror is a tactic that can be utilized in a variety of contexts, for a broad range of purposes, generated by a wide spectrum of motives. Thus terror is a component in many activities. The question then is how much space within a given activity is occupied by this component. In terrorism, unlike its neighboring reference categories (from state terror to guerrilla warfare), the terror component is the preeminent and preponderate component of the whole of which it is a part.

Whatever else is said about terrorism, its almost total concentration on targets of opportunity (i.e., the defenseless) provides it with its special distasteful flavor whether or not one seeks to justify its occurrence.

In his book *Political Terrorism,* Grant Wardlaw reminds us that, "A major stumbling block to the serious study of terrorism is that, at base, terrorism is a moral problem."[24] Different groups, with differing stakes and perspectives, therefore apply or reject the label accordingly. "One man's terrorist," in other words, "is another man's patriot." As Yassir Arafat stated in his 1974 United Nations speech, "He who fights for a just cause, he who fights for the liberation of his country, he who fights against invasion and exploitation or singlemindedly against colonialism, can never be defined a terrorist."[25]

This view, however, mistates the moral dimensions of the subject. It may be that under a given set of circumstances, an individual or group is entitled to violently break some eggs in order to make a just omelette. But what eggs are chosen and the method in which they are broken are never outside the realm of proper moral judgments. Just cause or not, he who performs acts of terrorism is a terrorist. And because terrorism violates the norms associated with the discriminating and proportional use of violence, it leaves itself open to moral condemnation regardless of its results and its political orientations.[26]

In a thoughtful essay on "Motives, Means and Consequences," Joseph Nye, Jr. notes that, "No formula can solve a moral dilemma."[27] In a similar vein, one might argue that no definition can solve the dilemma connected to terrorism when terrorism is seen as a moral problem. Yet this does not mean that no alternative exists to the "terrorist/patriot" cliche.

It is possible to avoid "one dimension ethics" and still render meaningful moral judgments.[28] In this regard, judgments need to invoke the multiple dimensions of motives, means and consequences. As a philosophy of means, terrorism is subject to judgment based on means alone. At the same time, the judgment on means may be shaded (but not eliminated) by the consideration of motives and consequences.

Thus we come full circle, back to the question of definition. Without an unambiguous definition, is the use of the term nothing more than an exercise in advocacy, a verdict rooted solely in social judgment?[29] Here it is worth considering a comment made by Potter Stewart in 1964. Seven years after the United States Supreme Court first entered the murkey waters of obscenity, the late justice said this about hard-core ponography:

> I shall not attempt further to define the kinds of
> material I understand to be embraced within that short-
> hand description and perhaps I could never succeed in
> intelligibly doing so. But I do know it when I see it, and
> the motion picture involved in this case is not that.[30]

In terms of distinguishing the phenomenon in question (hard-core pornography) from related phenomena, Stewart's words clearly fail to offer a sufficiently coherent and constant statement (definition) allowing for a purely logical and rational application of the term in specific and varying circumstances. But despite this definitional barrier, Stewart's "I do know it when I see it" comment should not be viewed as a completely arbitrary or capricious exercise. Stewart, in essence, was dealing with pornography the way Bowyer Bell has dealt with terror, as ". . . a condition known implicitly to most men, but which is somehow beyond rigorous examination."[31] This implicit knowledge is not a matter of whim, but of agreement (articulated or not) on the critical elements that constitute the core of each activity.

From this perspective, the debate over definition is less significant than the debate over the propriety of the action, that is its morality. Opponents and defenders of pornography do not really disagree over what constitutes the phenomenon. Instead, the debate really centers on its acceptability under given sets of circumstances. Seen in this light, the search for greater definitional finality is "like the anti-hero in a lost generation novel, looking for God in the wrong places."[32]

Such is also the case with terrorism. Take away the emotive connotations of the term and the definitional disagreements rapidly fade in significance. Ultimately, as a moral matter, terrorism is perhaps best approached in the same way a French peasant spoke in the 16th century of the religious wars in that country: "Who will believe that your cause is just when your behaviors are so unjust?"[33]

No matter what the terrors of definition, that query can never be ignored.

Notes

[1]J. Bowyer Bell, *A Time of Terror* (New York: Basic Books, 1978), p. ix.

[2]Tony Geraghty, "Introduction" in Royal United Services Institute for Defence Studies, *Ten Years of Terrorism* (New York: Crane, Russak and Company, 1979), p. 4. The late 1960s represents the time period generally used to mark the beginning of modern terrorism; see, for example, Walter Laqueur's *Terrorism* (Boston: Little, Brown and Company, 1977), Chapter Five, "Terrorism Today."

[3]Baljit Singh, "Overview" in Yonah Alexander and Seymour Maxwell Finger (eds.), *Terrorism: Interdisciplinary Perspectives* (New York: The John Jay Press, 1977), p. 6. Walter Laquer (ed.), *The Terrorism Reader* (New York: New American Library, 1978) has as its first reading an excerpt from Aristotle, *Politics* Book V on "The Origin of Tyranny," pp. 10-13.

[4]Alex Schmid, *Political Terrorism* (New Brunswick: Transaction Books, 1983), p. 39. Also, see M. Cherif Bassiouni, "The Origins and Fundamental Causes of International Terrorism" in Bassiouni (ed.), *International Terrorism and Political Crimes* (Springfield, Illinois: Charles C. Thomas, 1975), p. 6. There Bassiouni writes of the evolution in the ordinary meaning of the term terrorism since its emergence at the end of the 18th century: "While at first it applied mainly to those acts and policies of governments which were designed to spread terror among a population for the purpose of ensuring its submission to and conformity with the will of those governments, it now seems to be mainly applied to actions by individuals, or groups of individuals."

[5]Augustus Norton and Martin Greenberg, *International Terrorism: An Annotated Bibliography and Research Guide* (Boulder: Westview Press 1980) and Edward Mickolus, *The Literature of Terrorism: A Selectively Annotated Bibliography* (Westport, Connecticut: Greenwood Press, 1980).

[6]J. Bowyer Bell, *Transnational Terror* (Stanford: Hoover Institution, 1975), Hoover Institution Studies 53, p. 6, published jointly with The American Enterprise Institute.

[7]J. Bowyer Bell, "Trends in Terror," *World Politics,* Vol. 29, No. 3 (April 1977), 481.

[8]Jordan Paust, "A Definitional Focus" in Alexander and Finger (eds.), *Terrorism*, p. 19.

[9]Schmid, *Political Terrorism.*

[10]Schmid, *Political Terrorism,* pp. 73-75.

[11]Schmid, *Political Terrorism,* p. 8.

[12]Brian Jenkins and Janera Johnson, *International Terrorism: A Chronology, 1968-1974,* a report prepared for the Department of State and Defense Advanced Research Projects Agency, R-1597-DOSIARPA (March 1975) published by Rand Corporation, Santa Monica, California. Edward Mickolus, *Codebook: Iterate* (Ann Arbor: Inter-University Consortium for Political and Social Research, 1976). Also, see Mickolus, "An Events Data Base for Studying Transnational Terrorism: in Richards Heuer, Jr. (ed), *Quantitative Approaches to Political Intelligence: The CIA Experience* (Boulder: Westview Press, 1978).

[13]Jenkins and Johnson, *International Terrorism,* p. 3.

[14]"Mickolus, *Codebook: Iterate,* cited by Schmid, *Political Terrorism,* p. 258.

[15]Schmid, *Political Terrorism,* pp. 76-77. Compare with, Gaston Bouthal, "Definitions of Terror" in David Carlton and Carlo Schaerf (eds), *International Terrorism and World Security* (New York: John Wiley, 1975), pp. 51-53 and Paust "A Definitional Focus" in Alexander and Finger (eds), pp. 18-19.

[16]Schmid, *Political Terrorism,* p. 110.

[17]Schmid, *Political Terrorism,* p. 111.

[18]Schmid, *Political Terrorism,* pp. 79-96, offers a detailed examination of such distinctions.

[19]Frederick Hacker, *Crusaders, Criminals, Crazies* (New York: Bantam Books, 1978).

[20]On "The Semantics of 'Terror,'" see Noam Chomsky and Edward Herman, *The Washington Connection and Third World Fascism,* Volume One (Boston: South End Press, 1979), pp. 6-7. Compare with Alex Schmid and Janny de Graff *Violence as Communication* (New York: Sage, 1982), p. 2, which relates the insurgency/state terror difference to the publicity component.

[21]Fifty percent of the respondents to Schmid's questionnaire believed state terror should be included in the term terrorism, Schmid, *Political Terrorism*, p. 103.

[22]Schmid, *Political Terrorism*, p. 66.

[23]Louis René Beres, *Apocalypse* (Chicago: University of Chicago Press, 1982), p. 110.

[24]Grant Wardlaw, *Political Terrorism* (Cambridge: Cambridge University Press, 1982), p. 4.

[25]Cited in Schmid, *Political Terrorism*, p. 100.

[26]James Turner Johnson, *Can Modern War Be Just?* (New Haven: Yale University Press, 1984) pp. 60-63 and Beres, *Apocalypse*, p. 118.

[27]Joseph Nye, Jr., "Motives, Means and Consequences," *Society*, Vol. 22, No. 3 (March/April 1985), 18.

[28]Nye, "Motives," 18.

[29]See Luigi Bonante and J. Bowyer Bell cited by Schmid, *Political Terrorism*, p. 7.

[30]*Jacobellis v. Ohio* 378U.S.184 at 197.

[31]J. Bowyer Bell, *Transnational Terrorism*, p. 6.

[32]R. Schroth, review of *The Death and Life of Bishop Pike* in The New York Times, *Book Review*, August 1, 1976, 3.

[33]Cited by Johnson, *Can Modern War*, p. 61.

The Rationality of Terrorism

2

ROBERT MARANTO

Introduction

Terrorists are typically viewed as romantic idealists or mindless predators. Rationality based approaches to terrorist behavior have correspondingly not been attempted. Terrorist movements vary greatly in composition, objectives and strategy. Yet terrorism, like more conventional warfare, can be understood as politics pursued by other means. Accordingly, political economic models of international conflict can be applied to the strategies of terrorist alliances, albeit with diminished empirical utility owing to the shadowy character and small numbers of their quarry.

Since Mancur Olson's pioneering work in the mid 1960's, the economic theory of collective (or "public") goods has been used with varying success to describe all sorts of political activity and inactivity. Olson and others have often treated the international security provided by peacetime alliances as a collective good. Yet these scholars have not applied their frameworks to the fighting conducted when alliances are actually employed in wartime; nor have they considered the special problems nonstate alliances have in collectively waging their conflicts. This paper will briefly outline the collective goods paradigm and its previous employment in studies of defense policy. Further, we will suggest how these concepts could describe terrorist movements.

Collective Goods

In his seminal *The Logic of Collective Action,* Mancur Olson develops the collective goods approach previously suggested by Head, Musgrave, Samuelson, and other economists. Olson applies the concept to such behavior as political lobbying, the formation of labor unions, international alliance behavior, and even the revolution of the proletariat.[1]

Purely collective (or public) goods can be distinguished from private goods by their nonexclusivity and nonrivalness. Private goods are exclusive and rival since the consumer of a particular good can exclude others from its consumption and since his or her consumption leaves a smaller quantity of the good to be consumed by others. For example, a consumer's purchase of a Cabbage Patch Doll, given a (perhaps artificially) limited supply of the good, leaves one less doll to be enjoyed by others. The consumer, moreover, can and probably will exclude others from using his or her doll. National defense, in contrast, is consumed equally by all within a polity (though not all may desire the same amount of defense) and none can be deprived of its

I wish to thank the Office of Research at the University of Southern Mississippi for its support of this project. I wish to thank Joseph R. Goldman for his insight.

benefits. The supply is similarly nonrival since the addition of an individual to the polity and his or her consumption of its defense does not leave less of the good to be enjoyed by others.

Since none can be excluded, all within a polity will benefit from the provision of a collective good whether or not they contribute their share to cost of the good. In a large community, moreover, an individual's contribution to the provision of a collective good will have no recognizable impact on its supply and hence provide little strictly utilitarian incentive for the individual to contribute. This is not to say that nonmaterial, or in economic parlance, "nonrational" incentives are not important.[2] Still, in these large or "latent" groups, many will free ride, enjoying the benefits of the collective good without paying their fair share for it. Olson therefore argues that collective goods provided by and for large communities will normally be provided in a severely suboptimal quantity (and may not be provided at all) unless individuals are coerced to contribute or given selective incentives only available to those who do contribute.[3] Mandatory taxation is an example of the former. The magazines, special insurance policies, trips, and other selective incentives offered to members of unions and various lobbying organizations are examples of the latter. Apparently, few farmers, factory workers, or others will join organizations which could yield their groups great benefits unless they are coaxed by selective incentives or intimidated in various ways some not unlike terrorism.

This simple understanding leads to interesting propositions about actor size and organization formation. Most important, large actors may have sufficient incentive to provide a collective good benefiting many others simply because they have so much at stake and since their resources are sufficient to provide all or most of the cost of the good. For example, Olson and Zeckhauser found that the larger members of the NATO alliance bore a disproportionate share of the cost of the common defense. The large had less to gain from driving a hard bargain and more to lose from withdrawal.[4]

Other researchers have extended this analysis, finding that different types of NATO defense expenditures are more or less collective in nature and accordingly more or less susceptible to the free-riding of the small. For example, the airports, roads, and other infrastructure costs of the alliance provide many distinctly national benefits. It is therefore not surprising that the small members of NATO fully shoulder their fair share of these burdens.[5]

The Political Economics of Fighting Alliances

Despite the various applications of collective goods theory to alliance behavior, none have applied the paradigm to the actual fighting conducted when alliances are employed in wartime. This is largely because victory in war, unlike national defense in peacetime, is a good so highly valued that any increase in national income will be devoted to its provision.[6] Within very loosely joined or even essentially hostile alliances systems, very different processes may be at work. Within these alliances, the exhaustion of allies may be a good valued nearly so highly as the eventual defeat of the collective foe. Free-riding might occur, for some members will make calculated effort to allocate a disproportionate share of the costs of the conflict to their allies. For example, revisionist historians have suggested that the Anglo-American refusal to set up a second front against the Nazis until late in World War II reflects a deliberate effort to bleed the Red Army white in its struggle against the Germans and thereby facilitate the Anglo-American domination of postwar Europe.[7]

Our previous theoretical work suggests that such tendencies may be pronounced within guerrilla alliances or other alliances composed of nonstate actors. Nonstate allies are particularly unlikely to be well united in the pursuit of victory. If they are essentially revolutionary rather than nationalist movements, they will lack an acceptable prewar status quo from which to gain precedents for the postwar distribution of stakes. All the rebels are after the total control of the same government, and in the past many fully successful revolutions have served as a prelude to a far bloodier struggle determining who holds final power.[8] It has been suggested that Lenin had this in mind when he held back his Bolshevics from participating in the March 1917 revolution against the Czar. He thereby conserved his forces while the Liberals lost troops in the revolution, leaving themselves ripe for defeat in the fall.[9]

In extreme cases, one coalition member could even betray another. For example, it has been suggested that during the Vietnamese revolution against France, the Communist Party gave the French secret police a list of Nationalist Party leaders, even though the Communists and Nationalists were loosely allied at the time.[10]

Terrorism and Guerrilla Conflict

In our previous work we have suggested that, particularly within guerrilla alliances, collective warmaking can be seen as a collective good subject to the free-riding common to such goods. The same may not be quite so true of terrorist alliances.

Terrorism is often thought of as guerrilla war; indeed, the two terms are often employed interchangeably. In contemporary debate it is typically assumed that both are modern conflicts waged by revolutionary forces using hit and run tactics to wear down and eventually defeat the superior forces of the reactionary state. In fact, both guerrilla war and terrorism date back to ancient times. The Chinese empire faced essentially guerrilla war in defeating peasant revolts as early as the Fourth Century B.C.. The Jewish Maccabees fought a successful guerrilla war against the Syrians in the Second Century B.C., and the Roman Empire defeated guerrilla movements undertaken at various times by the Jews, North Africans, and Celtiberians.[11] Similarly, Rapoport notes that the Zealots-Sicarii employed terrorism against the Romans and moderate Jewish leaders in the First Century A.D., and the Thugs have used terror against individuals for thousands of years.[12] Moreover, no ideology holds a monopoly on either strategy. Skilled guerrillas now fight Marxist regimes in Angola and Afghanistan, and one of the most successful (though losing) guerrilla struggles of all time was fought against the French Revolutionary government by the rightist peasants and nobles of the Vendee region. The Black Hundreds, Nazis, KKK, and other reactionary groups have with varying success employed terrorism or spawned terrorist movements.

What then, are these phenomena? Guerrilla warfare denotes tactics employed by forces which cannot profitably meet the enemy in a conventional battle because they are outgunned. The guerrillas therefore employ relatively small scale assaults on weak enemy positions, fequently disbursing after an attack. Their very weakness dictates a larely nocturnal strategy most active in remote regions where forests or rough terrain hinder the dominate army in its search and destroy missions. Successful guerrilla forces develop "liberated zones" under their authority. These regions serve symbolic purposes, provide training grounds, supply food and other materials, and give fighters a refuge. Victorious guerrilla forces (and few are victorious) must eventually form units large enough to fight conventional battles. Guerrillas can never defeat a determined enemy without reaching this stage.[13]

Terrorism denotes the killings, bombings, robberies, kidnappings, hijackings, and other destructive acts committed by small groups or individuals aimed at overthrowing or influencing the regime.[14] (Notably, some of these activities, particularly robberies, can also help keep the terrorists in business.) Terrorism may be employed against specific targets linked to the offending regime or movement. Just as typically it is employed at random, to undermine regime authority by making it clear that the government cannot protect its citizens.[15]

Terrorism may act as adjunct to a guerrilla movement. For example, the Viet Cong quietly assassinated thousands of South Vietnamese village leaders in the 1950's and 1960's to remove the indigenous nonCommunist leadership.[16] Terrorism cannot on its own win power however, for by definition terrorism employs forces far too small to directly combat the state. Notwithstanding current speculation about nuclear terrorism and the optimistic Narodnaya Volya belief that government would fall if a few leaders were eliminated, terrorism has never toppled a regime by itself. The most it has managed has been to help make liberal democracies less liberally democratic or (usually unintentionally) helped authoritarians overthrow such relatively benign regimes. The highly active leftist Uruguayan and Argentine terrorists of the 1970's, for example, only succeeded in provoking rightist military coups against the rather democratic governments of their nations. The new military regimes then fought ruthless (and successful) "dirty wars" against the terrorist movements.[17]

The Rational Terrorist

Terrorist acts may be motivated by material or purposive incentives. (Terrorist groups are often held together by social ties, yet these incentives do not in and of themselves require terrorist acts for fulfillment.) As Laqueur details, many modern day terrorists are sponsored by governments. Libya, Iraq, Iran, South Yeman and various other states have subsidized

14

terrorists or even paid for them to handle specific jobs. The infamous "Carlos" and certain other terrorists and terrorist trainers are distinguished by their Swiss bank accounts and other benefits provided by governments who make use of their skills in furthering national foreign policy goals and enhancing international prestige. Such a nominal world power as Libya, for example, has gained considerable influence by sponsoring various movements.[18] While normally motivated at least partly by ideological concerns, it can be suggested that these terrorists are as much mercenaries as freedom fighters.

International terrorists employed or supported by governments can find refuge within those nations. Even if apprehended, they may well serve only a few years provided that they ply their trade within relatively liberal states.[19] Terrorism can therefore offer good employment for the utility minded soldier.

These relatively utilitarian terrorists may work together with other groups at times. Yet profiteering fighters are apt to lack a meaningful long term program separate from that of their sponsors. Arrangements between these terrorist groups will therefore be set up to tackle a single act in a contractual manner rather than to independently conduct an allied campaign against the same enemy state. The respective inputs of personnel for each act are thus known. Ironically, free-riding among such groups is therefore not possible, at least partly because of the rationality of the terrorists and calculability of inputs, outputs, and inducements.

More typical terrorists are motivated by essentially purposive aims. This is particularly true of those operating within a single authoritarian or totalitarian state. Such terrorism holds great risks and no material rewards save the occasional take from a bank heist or kidnapping. Even then, repressive governments are apt to treat anti-state robbers far more harshly than common criminals, making politically justified crime a far riskier profession. Of course, this is not always the case in more liberal states. Indeed, in these nations apprehended terrorists may be treated more humanely than ordinary criminals since it is assumed that they acted for reasons more noble than personal gain. In addition, since liberal states see nonviolent pressures as legitimate, they may also view violent political activity in a more restrained fashion than nonliberal states and may even give in to certain pressures in hope of buying them off in the same manner that nonviolent pressure groups can be pleased. For some purposively motivated terrorists, terror is an end in itself. Indian Thugs, for example, killed as a religious sacrifice to Kali, who derived satisfaction from the suffering of the victim and dedication of the murderer.[20] More recently, Fanon has suggested that the mere act of violence against an "oppressor" is emotionally liberating.[21] In addition, it must be suggested that at least some terrorists derive pleasure from the adventure of their activity. For participants with these primary motivations, no coalition partners are necessary. If coalitions do occur, no partner will seek to avoid activity, for participation itself is the goal, whatever its cost. Similarly, these groups are unlikely to be appeased by inducement offers from their targets, for their aims are by nature intangible.

Terrorism is more typically employed as a means to the end of altering government policy (as in anti-abortion bombings or bombings protesting American involvement in Vietnam) or eventually taking power by destroying the government leaders or mass confidence in them. This basic proposition has important implications for the political economy of terrorism. First, those protesting particular policies can often be appeased by concessions, particularly if the sacred policies are singular in nature and not linked to a broad ideology. Further, even in relatively liberal states where terrorists are not likely to meet death or torture, those so determined as to employ terrorism are either abherent personalities, or, more often, motivated by deeply help ideals which tolerate little deviation. Either way, it is not surprising that broad terrorist "movements" (e.g., the PLO, the IRA, the Weathermen and Yippies, etc.) are typically well splintered alliances of narrow factional groups. This has implications for coalitional behavior within such alliances, for free-riding or even betrayal to the state authorities can be expected.

In radical perspectives, free-riders are moderates who choose less risky (and less violent) means of carrying out the struggle against the regime. For example, in the Introduction to his *Terrorism and Communism* Trotsky condemns the followers of Kautsky, who refrains from and advises against violent revolutionary action. Though not always in support of terrorism, Lenin similarly attacks the Mensheviks for their moderation in the struggle.[22] Similar denunciations of moderates have been made by rightist and nationalist terrorists. In the eyes of radicals, violent action is necessary for meaningful change. Those individuals and groups which do not assist in terrorism and revolt are simply free-riding off the efforts of others by avoiding the risky contributions to social transformation while being perfectly ready to benefit from it if it comes to pass.[23]

Betrayal is of a somewhat different character. It can be suggested that the aforementioned hostility extremist groups hold for their natural allies encourages betrayal to the authorities. For example, factions within the broad Armenian ASALA terrorist organization regularly betray other factions to Western authorities and even engage in acts of terror against them.[24] The Vietnamese case mentioned above can also be cited, and it is hardly surprising that terrorist groups confide little in their allies even where police penetration is not feared. In other instances moderate supporters of the cause may betray terrorists to reach accommodation with the regime or because they themselves fear the extremists. In a somewhat different vein, it can be suggested that terrorists may wish the destruction of other antigovernment groups since those groups compete for followers during the struggle and could well compete for power should the antigovernment activity ever succeed.[25] Given these incentives for betrayal, it is not surprising that a determined and united secret police or military can generally learn a great deal about a terrorist group and destroy it. As Laqueur's work notes time and time again, terrorists operating within a single regime, particularly an oppressive one, usually have short life spans whatever their level of popular support or ideological merit. This seems less true of ethnic groups than of fundamentally ideological ones, perhaps because ideological motivations are inherently more subject to disagreement (and corresponding problems of collective action) and less apt to gain widespread support.

It can be suggested that Marxist theory, at least, takes some notice of these factors. Communist political and military organizations attempt to gain dominance over their leftist (and other) allies and integrate them into a "united front" before fully pressing the battle against the government.[26] As Marx's reflections about the Paris Commune make clear, he distrusted allies and was keenly aware of the difficulties of coordinating a proletariat represented by more than one organization.[27] Lenin's views on the subject have already been noted, and the united front strategy could be interpreted as a means to eliminate rational free-riding or betrayal on the part of allies.

Conclusion

Political Economic approaches hold considerable power in explaining the micro level organization of interests. In addition, these analyses have been usefully employed to describe the behavior of international military alliances operating in peacetime. Political economic thinking has not been used to analyze fighting alliances, but we maintain that under certain circumstances nations and organizations will free-ride off their allies in collective warmaking. This is particularly true of the nonstate alliances employing terrorism or fighting guerrilla wars.

From our standpoint, terrorism differs most from guerrilla war in its smaller probability of winning power. It is not surprising that many terrorists---some of them essentially mercenaries---are not clearly after taking over government. This is important since the incentives which drive terrorists have implications for combatting them. For example, if nations band together to liquidate mercenary terrorists even within their sponsor states, this activity will no longer offer adequate economic rewards and will probably diminish. Of course, such anti-terrorist activity can itself be considered a collective good subject to considerable free-riding on the part of nations. Moreover, such activity is unlikely to succeed so long as a large number of states tacitly approve of (even if they do not support) terrorists with foreign policy goals congruent to their own.

Other terrorists are motivated by the thrill of action or the joy of violence against an "oppressor." Again, more aggressive pursuit of terrorists could have some deterrent effect. Yet the nature of these motivations suggests that these forms of terrorism will be difficult to stop since the act of terror is an end in itself rather than a means to make money or alter policy.

Perhaps most typically, terrorists use their acts as a means to an ideological end. In these cases, moderates can often be coopted or convinced to leave the struggle and betray radicals to the regime (or at least "free-ride" off their violent cohorts) if certain concessions are granted them even as the state acts aggressively against the terrorists. Even when there are no moderates, the splintered nature of militant ideological organizations suggests that factions will often betray their allies, or at least

17

not greatly assist other groups under attack. The regime should, and usually does, foster the various divisions among these groups. Unfortunately (or maybe not), nationalist movements are far less likely to suffer the divisions of ideological organizations. This, combined with their mass base, makes them more difficult to repress.

Notes

[1]Olson, Mancur (1971) *The Logic of Collective Action*. Cambridge: Harvard University Press.

[2]Hardin, Russell (1982) *Collective Action*. Baltimore: John Hopkins University Press. In Particular, see Chapter Seven.

[3]Olson, *Op. Cit.* In particular, see the first two chapters.

[4]Olson, Mancur, and Richard Zeckhauser (1966) "An Economic Theory of Alliances," *Review of Economics and Statistics* 48:266-79.

[5]Sandler, Todd M. (1977) "Impurity of Defense: An Application to the Economics of Alliances," *Kyklos* 30:443-60.

[6]Olson and Zeckhauser, *Op. Cit.* p. 270.

[7]Ambrose, Stephen (1983) *Rise to Globalism*. New York: Penquin.

[8]These themes are explored in somewhat greater depth in "To the Victor Goes the Spoils: Collective Action Theory and Guerrilla War," by Robert Maranto and Joseph R. Goldman, presented at the 1985 Midwest Political Science Association Convention in Chicago.

[9]This case is described in two notable books. Alexander Rabinowitch (1976) penned *The Bolshevics Come to Power: The Revolution of 1917 in Petrograd*, New York: Norton. Leonard Schapiro (1983) wrote *The Russian Revolutions of 1917: The Origins of Modern Communism*, New York: Basic.

[10]Pike, Douglas (1978) *A History of Vietnamese Communism*. Stanford: Hoover Institution Press.

[11]See, for example, the first chapter of John Ellis' (1975) *A Short history of Guerrilla War*, New York: St. Martin's.

[12]Rapoport, David C. (1984) "Fear and Trembling: Terrorism in Three Religious Traditions," *American Political Science Review* 78:658-77.

[13]Galula, David (1964) *Counterinsurgency Warfare: Theory and Practice*. New York: Praeger.

[14]Latin American death squads and analogous groups elsewhere are often referred to as "state terorists." Such a designation is quite reasonable, but presents a topic largely beyond the scope of this paper.

[15]Laqueur, Walter (1977) *Terrorism*. Boston: Little, Brown and Company, Chapter Two.

[16]Pike, Douglas (1969) *War, Peace, and the Viet Cong*. Cambridge: MIT Press. p. 64.

[17]Laqueur, *Op. Cit.*, pp. 186-7.

[18]*Ibid.*, Chapter Five.

[19]*Ibid.*

[20]Rapoport, *Op. Cit.*

[21]Fanon, Frantz (1966) *The Wretched of the Earth*. New York: Grove Press.

[22]Lenin, V.I. (1951) *Marx Engels Marxism*. Moscow: Foreign Languages Publishing House. pp. 186-99.

[23]This is a common theme in the microanalytic rational choice approaches to revolution. For a good summary, see Morris Silver's (1974) "Political Revolution and Repression: An Economic Approach," *Public Choice* 17:63-71.

[24]Gunter, Michael M. (1985) "Armenian Terrorism Today: Analysis or Autopsy?" presented at the 1985 Southern Political Science Association Convention in Nashville. See pages 1-7.

[25]Maranto and Goldman, *Op. Cit.*

[26]Galula, *Op. Cit.* pp. 46-8.

[27]Teplov, F. and V. Davydov (1978) *The Socialist Revolution*. Moscow: Progress Publishers. In particular, see pages 68-9 and 312.

Irrational Terrorism

3

BERNARD SCHECHTERMAN

Efforts at defining and classifying recent international terrorism overwhelmingly focus on *politically motivated behavior* as both the causal factor and goal for such activities. These activities usually take the form of state terrorism, state-sponsored terrorism, or revolutionary terrorism. Simply stated, state terrorism is a government's abuse of its own people. Frequently such abuse comes under the heading of human rights violations by a regime in its own jurisdiction. State-sponsored terrorism involves a specific government providing the wherewithal (arms, finances, training, transport, sanctuary, inspirational values) to like-minded groups or individuals with the avowed purposes of destabilizing another society. Ultimate goals may include replacing the societal leadership or values with those amenable to the sponsors. Revolutionary terrorism begins in indigenous groups or individuals seeking to alter or replace an existing regime, with or without outside support. Often, the ultimate aspiration may include the creation of a separate state based on earlier historical record or as a promise made in the past. The actual permutations in this latter category of terrorism are many, and often overlap with state-sponsored terrorism.

Whether or not one agrees with the above generalized characterizations, the clear implication is that politically motivated behavior is viewed as both rationally understandable and discernible (even if disapproved) so that it allows a calculated response. At best it implies the resolvability of such behavior when causal factors are remedied or removed; at its worst it implies the ability to cope with many of the negative aspects of such behavior through damage control efforts or more efficient reactions.

As vital as the inquiry into these more obvious forms of terrorism may be, investigation usually overlooks or inadequately confronts another variation, irrational terrorism, which is more disturbing by its very nature, and because of the ramifications for governments and individuals alike. This chapter will demonstrate the increasing need to understand this mushrooming phenomenon.

Distinguishing between politically motivated and irrational forms of terrorism is complicated by the tendency of authoritative elites facing threats to their societies (or groups therein) to assign political motivations to terroristic acts, even when the centrality of such attitudes may be lacking altogether. This simplification reassures authorities that they fully comprehend events that, in turn, will permit a meaningful response. Conveying an image of control to the home audience as well as to other governments has become a priority in the posturing of political elites in power. Categorizing behavior in popularly perceived terms avoids public panic and provides the appearance of an effective job performance. Since one of the objectives of many terrorists may well be to create an image of official uncertainty or ignorance, there is some urgency for governments to be specific; therefore, they classify behavior as politically motivated even when they are unsure or incorrect. However, it is increasingly likely that the overall political climate is being exploited by the irrational terrorist.

Broad Concepts

Conor Cruise O'Brien, in discussing popular versions of the international terrorist, cites two categories: the "misguided idealist," and the "unstable person."[1] His second category, approximate to my characterizations of irrational, includes the outright lunatic (he uses the popular term "nut"), the criminal-type thug, and a dupe of some clever state or movement. The first two of these unstable types may well fit into the more sophisticated characterizations of irrational terrorism developed in this chapter. (O'Brien's third type, the dupe, could also fit in, but without more detail and analysis the dupe could as well be politically motivated).

There are three general criteria for labeling terrorists and their acts irrational:

The terrorists' consistent failure to define or stress sought-after political goals in their public rhetoric. The best concrete indicator of such an orientation is the failure to declare and/or disseminate an explicit political program or objective to be attained as a result of the violent action. The frequent pattern is to assert the absolute priority of first bringing about an institutional change, which would then be followed by the concrete tasks of formulating and implementing political and other programs.

Simcha Jacobovici writes, "The political ends of terrorists are difficult to ascertain since by its very nature terrorism rejects politics. By opting for terror, terrorists demonstrate they are anti-political." He says further:

> The apocalyptic end always remains a vague, almost mystical vision. Whether the goal is held sincerely or not, it in no way challenges the organization's immediate programme. Asked what he foresaw for a free and united Ireland, Ruain O'Bradaigh of the IRA answered simply, "Who knows what happens when power is in the hands of the people." Sorel would have approved of O'Bradaigh. After all, Sorel approvingly attributes to Marx the statement, "The man who draws up a programme for the future is a reactionary." The ideology of terror leaves to personal idiosyncracies the vision of the end. Instead, it draws up a programme for the present.[2]

And there is little doubt that the immediate program focuses on the act of terror itself.

Often a corollary argument or rationale is proffered that the existing political system, even when presumably democratic by most people's standards, is unresponsive to their participation or general demands. Minimally, the terrorist always focuses on some change in an existing status quo, whether of personal or societal importance.

The above line of reasoning automatically legitimizes the terrorists' right to operate outside the existing rules (norms) and institutionalized modes of behavior in the society. The second criterion for labeling terrorists irrational is that *they can resort to their own defined (self-confirming) code of behavior.* In open or democratic societies this assertion or condemnation can be tested by scrutinizing the previous record of societal participation (or lack of it) of the personnel involved. With rare exception, the irrational terrorist has demonstrated a tendency to opt for violence as the first or only, rather than the ultimate course of action. With each succeeding violent act there emerges even less prospect of recourse to nonviolent modes of behavior to attain objectives.

The third criterion to classify the irrational terrorist is that for such people *the act of terrorism is in itself an ultimate satisfaction*. Inherent in the resort to violence is the consummation of a personality need, often an infatuation with the whole phenomenon. The depth and persistence of this psychological and circumstantial orientation is more pronounced for some groups and individuals, as indicated by the consistency of their attitudes and behavior over extended periods of time—we are talking about years versus weeks or months, although there are always exceptions.

It needs to be reiterated that in the broadest sense the irrational terrorist conveys the guise of being a "political causist," confusing the observer and the classifier. By carefully examining the respective worlds of the victim(s) and the perpetrator of terrorism, the superficiality of this rationalization can be discerned for what it really is—a disguise for highly personalistic motivations removed from the direct and substantive world of politics.

Conditional Factors

The variant of terrorism called irrational shares most of the background and circumstantial features of the politically motivated forms of terrorism. More often than not, it reduces to individual perceptions of and responses to a social environment and set of circumstances that impact almost everyone.

For the terrorist in general, there is an intellectual legacy that has evolved in recent history, and that creates and sustains a climate of ideas that justify the resort to violence. The nineteenth century is replete with anarchistic and nihilistic advocates, the most noteworthy being Georges Sorel and Mikhail Bakunin. Joined to the Marxist legacy that traverses the nineteenth and twentieth centuries via violence-oriented people like Lenin and Trotsky, a powerful tangent on how to dissent was widely established in western societies and in western-educated circles in the less-developed regions of the world. This development is best validated by the transition of Marxist and anarchistic views from West to East and South via Maoism and Guevarism respectively. Interestingly enough, despite Europe's own linear evolution of the violence option, the messenger role of Regis Debray and others reunited the underdeveloped regions with the oldest developed region—a full circle in the intellectual violence process.

A vital element of the intellectual's thought pattern is the commitment to negativism directed against the overall society, determining many of the particular moment responses. In developed and affluent societies this is commonly referred to as "the adversary culture." With the explosion of education among larger populations everywhere after World War II, the number and impact of intellectuals has substantially increased; more importantly, intellectual life has made some followers thoroughly critical of their societies. As Hofstadter summarizes it, the inner need for intellectuals to criticize leads to a kind of desperate seeking of public sympathy and ends up in a pose at best. The intellectuals convince themselves they are somehow morally on trial and that they need to prove themselves by a constant refrain of repudiation and destruction. Negativism, really a form of antiintellectualism, more and more gets equated with intellectual merit. Hofstadter's postwar intellectuals end up being alienated from their society. This view is supported by an array of commentators—Daniel Bell, Herman Kahn, Patrick Moynihan, Lionel Trilling, Edward Shils, and Edward Banfield, among others. To speak positively about one's society became an untenable position in the climate of "the adversary culture."[3]

The analogous situation has been ever-present to one degree or another in Europe and among the western-educated "idea people" in the underdeveloped regions. Though philosophical orientations, intellectual posturing, and pedantic debates represent no commitment to violence per se, the climate of negativism, fully blown, has had a damaging impact on generations of postwar youth, some clearly opting for violence as readily justified.

Earlier anarchists and nihilists were split between rhetoricians and activists, but recently more terrorists' resort to violence is seen as crucial to their identity and status. This may indicate the degree to which they may have been influenced by additional social forces around them, whether accurately perceived or not. Revolutionary dynamics in innovative technology and economic systems have produced great dislocations and anomie among vast populaces, and especially so among the elite of such societies. The universal challenge to older belief systems and institutions, the inability to comprehend changes, and the growing impersonalism involved has led, as in other moments in history, to severe resistance as part of the reaction. Major juncture points in civilization development or undoing produce severe crises of values and intense forms of response.[4] Terrorism has been a reactive pattern for many people under such duress.

Finally, a crucial factor in the rise to prominence of the terror instrument has been the evolution of modes of violent behavior over time. If violence is viewed as an ongoing component in human relationships, rather than as a moral consideration, it is clear that the eras of conventional warfare and, in turn, nuclear warfare, have been respectively organized, institutionalized, and for the most part deterred (with no guarantee over future breakdowns). As persons have devised counter-strategems and capabilities to deal with these forms of violence, it is not surprising that advocates of violence have turned to unconventional forms of warfare—first guerrilla warfare (liberation movements), and eventually to terrorism. It was especially self-evident to terrorists that their mode of behavior had not produced a remedial or deterrent strategem comparable to the more conventional, and even more destructive nuclear forms of warfare. This major void has been a crucial factor in evoking terrorism and sustaining it as well.

Variations in Irrational Terrorism

No priority is attached to the variations of irrational terrorism that are discussed in this chapter. Six categories are established, identified, and explained as: 1) terror as personality fulfillment, or transforming; 2) terror as hatred; 3) terror as majority acceptance; 4) terror as vengeance; 5) terror as nonpolitical power seeking; and 6) terror as "fad." In several of these instances the categories are sufficiently broad to include significant nuance variations that might call for additional distinctive classifications, but that is not within the scope of this chapter.

Terror as Personality Fulfillment

In identifying and explaining terror as personality fulfillment or transforming, a modern starting point could well be Karl Heinzen, author of *Der Mord* (*Murder,* 1849), who argued for personality (value) transformation as necessary to facilitate and sustain terroristic acts. After noting and attacking as fictional all the societal moralistic arguments about killing one's enemy, he recommended that terrorists remove the "moral horror" from such acts and use the instrument of terror lavishly in the interests of humanity (which he defended in vague terms). Heinzen hoped some day the art of killing would be developed to the highest possible degree. Terror was to be an expression of artistic personality as it became an art in itself.[5]

Another example of terror as personality fulfillment is Albert Camus's play, *Les Justes,* which revolves around two Russian assassins at the turn of the century. The conflict is between a politically motivated terrorist and a comrade with a vague notion of ends, but a vision of the act of terror as providing everything he seeks for personal fulfillment. In this play, love of humanity (in a positive but undefined sense) is to be strong enough to justify murdering innocent children. In both of the above examples, exercising a conscience is labeled as being totally unprincipled and should not be allowed to corrupt one's truer personality and behavior.[6]

Contemporary and clearer expressions of this viewpoint are found in André Malraux's *La Condition Humaine,* where he says, "The act of terrorism is very often a potent instrument of self-expression rather than just a means toward some political end." Professor Toni Negri, chief ideologue of the Italian Red Brigades, has gone so far as to describe the act of terror as one of erotic love: ". . . it fills me with feverish emotion, as if I were waiting for a lover. . . ." Paul Wilkinson, referring to this type of behavior as "the politics of the blood," says that in the end it leads to an amoral anesthetization of politics. Laurent Tailhade, hearing that an anarchist bomb had been thrown into the sitting French Chamber of Deputies, commented: "Qu'importe les victimes, si le geste est beau (What do the victims matter, if the gesture is beautiful)?"[7]

Although all of the above have been critical chronological and intellectual underpinnings for western European, U.S., and western-educated, Third-World terrorists, greater influence in the post–World War II era can be attributed to two contemporaries—Frantz Fanon, the Algerian psychiatrist, and Che Guevara, the Argentinian/Cuban physician and collaborator with Castro. Both have had immeasurable impact beyond the realm of their own narrow revolutionary and violent involvements, countless terrorist efforts having been inspired by their behavior and ideology.

Fanon, author of *Les Damnés de la Terre* (*The Wretched of the Earth*), lauded violence as creative, innocent, therapeutic. For the Algerian revolutionary, as well as others, he had an exacting message: "Violence is a cleansing force. It frees the native from his inferiority (colonial) complex." He went on to say: "Violence is man recreating himself . . . when his rage boils over, he rediscovers his lost innocence and he comes to know himself in that he himself creates his self." Fanon endorsed violence (terrorism too) as a handmaiden for personality transformation,

23

the so-called submissive or previously subordinated persons finally emancipating themselves through the act of bloodletting, thus enabling the establishment of new personalities. Aside from the vast slaughter of Algerians and Frenchmen that was condoned by such views, the ramifications—if accepted by the mass of humanity in the underdeveloped countries of the world as well as by minorities and under-class elements in developed countries—would be horrendous.

Che Guevara reflects another version of the practical applications and implications of "personality fulfillment." In his transmigration to Cuba and role in its successful revolution, he became even more infatuated with violence as an ulti-mate and personally satisfying activity. This view was reflected in his unwilling-ness to accommodate himself to Castro's needs to institutionalize and govern after the revolution. Instead, he clearly desired to find and foment "action" oppor-tunities consistent with a personality constantly needing new violent undertakings. Although his Bolivian effort emphasized "guerrilla warfare" and so-called "libera-tion movements," Che's general legacy was the value and priority of violent modes of behavior. His undoing in Bolivia may have contributed directly to the downgrading of "guerrilla warfare" in favor of "terrorism" as the preferred and more viable instrument of personal or politically-motivated fulfillment.[8]

Terror as Hatred

"Terror as hatred" can best be analyzed from the predominance of the terrorist's personality orientation. In this category hatred is an attitude associated with a total antipathy to the society because of individual personality disorders usually at-tributable to discernible events or circumstances in the terrorist's background. Hatred is not anger, and although it may emanate initially from some sense of deep frustration or desperation, these latter feelings are associated with passion and pain, which may rise and fall in intensity, or disappear. Hatred is evidenced by cold, calculating, dispassionate, no-possible-alternative types of behavior and a deliberate choice of violence, including innumerable instances of wanton destruc-tion. This type of terrorist simply accepts that violence is the solution to all prob-lems in society, because there no longer is an acceptable version of society. Under a well-defined civil order, rather than a society of disorder or gross uncertainties, such a person would likely be labeled a criminal socio- or psychopath. When terror is exercised because of hatred, it gratifies the individual, and it becomes a sustain-ing factor in self-identity.

Robin Wright, specialist in Lebanese and Palestinian affairs, identifies the background variables common to the development of such personalities and their violent behavior.[9] The interplay of Lebanese factions and sects, including the Palestinians, has gone through two distinct phases. Until 1976, the internal strife and its manifestations, in whatever form and by whatever group, were predicated on likely political expectations or outcomes (even if they were often unrealistic). Wright describes the Lebanese climate after 1976 as civil strife "being played out in car bombings, kidnappings, and other indiscriminate violence among rival sects." A second generation of antagonists, mostly children, has been reared in a commonplace world of extremism, socializing them into a climate of intergroup violence as an automatic means of dealing with each other. Aggressive behavior is not being suppressed or redirected in any way. A disturbing development in this setting is the growth of hatred-condoned violence shifting from primarily Islamic extremists to ethnic and other religious extremists found throughout the Middle East.

According to psychologist Rona Fields, a common phenomenon, "the rejuvenation of violence," is taking place in a widespread geographic area including Lebanon, Israel, Northern Ireland, and South Africa. In too many cases the characterization labels it "mindless violence."[10] The question of what caused the conflicts in the first place has little or no bearing on the newer (children's) generation, since they are blameless as to its beginning. If anything, they have become the victims and have chosen to project that role onto others. Their preoccupation is with the surrounding violent world where there are all sorts of groups fighting for physical survival, usually at each other's expense. In 1982, before the Israeli invasion of Lebanon, Beirut's environs were commanded by eighty-two separately organized militia and terror groups focused merely on controlling their own streets. Anyone from any other area was the enemy and subject to violent retribution.

Indiscriminate violence, once politically or religiously motivated, increasingly reflects unthinking behavior or outright hatred unconnected to rational goals. Indiscriminate violence practiced in the above-cited societies means that politics has become irrelevant to increasing segments of the populations, especially to the new generations of young people. Because of their youth, these "kiddie terrorists" will be around for a long time to come.

A frightening corollary aspect of "terror as hatred" is the increasing availability of "freelancers" or "mercenaries" for terrorist acts.[11] Some are completely void of group affiliations or political or ideological orientations. Personal bitterness or a preoccupation with the terror act itself leads them to offer their services to anyone willing to pay for their talents. The recent cases of Nezar Hindawi's London airport operation and his brother's (Ahmed Hasi) bombing of a German–Arab Friendship Club in West Germany point up the nature of this problem. Here were several Palestinian refugees, products of the Lebanese turmoil, seeking a patron (Syria) to adopt their services. For the brothers, political nuances and moral principles were secondary to terror as a professional activity directed broadly against some hated target. The fact that the actual concrete targets varied so significantly from one society to another is the best indication of the terrorists' lack of forethought and general antagonism toward something as vaguely defined as "the West" (Israel included).

If Syria and other states continue to sponsor mercenaries, they may be compelled to recognize the phenomenon of irrational terrorism, and especially to identify the practitioners of "terror as hatred." Such terrorists can be genuinely counterproductive if they are neither predictable or controllable, and can even turn on the sponsor.[12]

Among the oldest forms of hatred is the "self" variety, common to members of a ruling-class elite or other successful groups or individuals. Guilt feelings over one's own status relative to that of disadvantaged people in the social system can mushroom into an absolutist condemnation of the entire social order. When the level of castigation reaches self-hatred (a definite personality and value transformation), terror directed against the society can be one means of expressing this attitude. The phenomenon has been vividly described among U.S. intellectuals.[13]

The cases of Patty Hearst and the Weathermen Underground certainly approximated this situation. After being kidnapped by the Symbionese Liberation Army, a violence-oriented group, Patty Hearst became a willing and active member. The Weathermen group, many from wealthy and higher-educational backgrounds, developed a level of hatred for American society rarely seen in our history. Some members are just beginning to surface after some twenty years of opposition and antagonism to the system. The psychological mechanics of the transformation from affluence to violent assault on the society may still be debated, but it does not alter the fact that it has happened among the elite in the United States and in virtually every open (democratic) society at some time.

Terror as Majority Acceptance

"Terror as majority acceptance" refers to a social-psychological dynamic of the relationship of minorities to majority demographics and values. In many instances of an overwhelming ethnic and/or religious majority populace, minorities resort to various tactics to gain acceptance and integration into the main social fabric.

In some of the more explosive and violent areas of the world—especially the Middle East—this dynamic has frequently led Christian Arab elements to opt for terror or other violence to gain the approval and acceptance of Muslim Arab neighbors or majorities (being Christian is looked upon as a form of civilization betrayal). There is the embarrassing (for the Vatican) case of the Palestinian Greek Catholic prelate, Archbishop Capucci, caught smuggling illegal arms across the Israeli-Lebanon border for the PLO, despite numerous warnings given him by Israeli authorities. Since that event, even the Holy See has had difficulty reining in the persistent extremist views and behavior of the prelate.

Two other perfect examples of the minority-majority dynamic are seen in Dr. George Habash and Naif Hawatmeh, Palestinian Christian leaders of two of the more extreme Palestine Liberation Organization affiliates—the Palestine Front for the Liberation of Palestine and the Democratic Front for the Liberation of Palestine, respectively. Both men seem to have to be more extreme and violent than their fellow Muslim Arabs in order to prove their credentials; they sustain their acceptance by adopting the purest (absolutist) party line of opposition to Israel and the West. Both reflect as well the upper-class upbringing so common to the "terror as hatred" group found among some of the affluent in the region and elsewhere.

A recent example is even more complex: George Abdallah, currently incarcerated in France for twin terror murders, came from a singular Christian village in southern Lebanon entirely surrounded by Muslim Shi'a villages and Palestinian Sunni refugee camps. The general region was dominated by a constant climate of violence directed against each other or Israel or both (analogous to the "terror as hatred" model). It has never been conclusively established whether Abdallah is a Greek Catholic or Greek Orthodox, but the distinction does not really matter in the dynamics of the case. Abdallah and other young men from his village joined a politically motivated Palestinian terrorist cell that collapsed when the Muslim leader died. He then took it upon himself to reorganize and activate the terrorist cell to prove his worth to the PLO. It was on one of his dangerous missions—to murder an American military officer and an Israeli official in France—that he was captured, nearly released, and finally held on the basis of "smoking-gun" evidence. The second part of Abdallah's terrorist career can only be understood as an effort to ingratiate himself with the major groups monopolizing the terrorist trade, who also happened to be almost exclusively Muslim.

Terror as Vengeance

The George Abdallah case also affords an opportunity to examine the category of "terror as vengeance." Although the concept of vengeance is not exclusive to any distinct culture or civilization, it is a deep-rooted one in the Arab/Islamic worlds of the Middle East. In this region the family, clan, or tribe evokes an extreme loyalty difficult to comprehend in more impersonal societies where the concept as a common or overriding form of behavior has long been absent. In Abdallah's case, however, once he was captured and awaiting trial, the social-psychological dynamic of vengeance came into play as a means of freeing him. His brothers, other family members, and other villagers immediately set out to retrieve him, according to the time-honored code of behavior. A series of terrorist attacks began in France, whose government alleged they were carried out by the extended family members. The goal was analogous to tribal vengeance in that such pressure could be built up to force their relative's release. Abdallah's original motivation for terror had been transformed from a political one to a personalized loyalty demanding family vengeful violence in order to gain his freedom. (Abdallah was tried for murder in 1987, and sentenced to life imprisonment.)

In one of the least-understood examples of the same dynamic at work, there is the case of the U.S. hostages held in the Bekaa Valley (Baalbeck) region of eastern Lebanon by Islamic radical fundamentalists. Although multiple motives underlie this hostage situation, the most consistent one has been a "family connection." Both the Islamic Amal and the Islamic Resistance Front, radical Shi'a groups sponsored and supported by Iran, are led by Husain Mussavi in the Bekaa Valley. Arch foes of Israel, the West, and some of the moderate Arab states in the Persian Gulf, three of Mussavi's family members are among seventeen prisoners being held in Kuwait because of a failed terrorist attempt. Since that attempt, innumerable terrorist acts have been perpetrated to pressure Kuwait and third parties into releasing the seventeen, but most particularly Mussavi's relatives. Seizing the U.S. hostages and holding them on Mussavi's turf in Lebanon was vengeance-motivated terror tactics of retaliation or reprisal.

The disappearance (and presumed death) of the Imam Musa Sadr, the crucial Lebanese Shi'a leader of the 1960s and 1970s in Libya at the hands of Qaddafi has produced several terror acts against Libyan officials. Two Lebanese Shi'a terrorists are now jailed in Spain because of their vengeful killing of Libyan representatives to that country.[14] Certainly one of the objectives of the terrorist acts was to force Libya to explain the Imam's disappearance but it would be foolish to ignore the intense hatred and desire for an "eye-for-an-eye" vindication sought by the Lebanese Shi'a community vis-à-vis the Qaddafi regime.

Terror as Nonpolitical Power Seeking

When venturing into the concept of "terror as nonpolitical power seeking," the task of documentation is more difficult than its identification and explanation. Power seeking under any circumstance involves several attitudes towards human relationships. There is a usual desire to seek and gain the attention of others. Acts of terror are often viewed as glamorous, especially in view of the major publicity given such events. There is a strong feeling of authority, control, and influence over a situation. The power of dominating or subordinating others (victims) stirs intense emotions in many terrorists. In an important sense, terror is enjoyable and self-fulfilling for the perpetrator because it provides such a commanding height in a particular setting of one's own choice. Despite invocations of generalized terms such as "the masses," "humanity," "the social system," or "the capitalist system," the terrorist who is power-seeking is truly an elitist. Because of a self-perception, as well as personality need, that identifies the act of terrorism as something unique and special, in the final analysis the power-seeking terrorist is antidemocratic, antimasses, and, above all, a totalitarian elitist.

The power-seeking terrorists are usually vague and almost flippant about resorting to terrorism for any purpose, perhaps because there is no serious expectation of attaining power. They often exhibit a detached attitude, even if the operations and impact are quite serious. Shirley Christian sees the Tupamaros of Uruguay as "[the] radicalization of a typical bourgeois sector—pseudo-intellectual—that one day said, 'Let's have a revolution here.'"[15] Despite their claims that Uruguay was a repressive society, it was a full-blown democracy before and during their terrorist onslaughts. Repression came as a response to their extensive use of urban terror, and only after they were caught and imprisoned. The military took over in 1973, in a society totally unprepared for political warfare. Since the return to democratic rule in March 1985, the Tupamaros, operating openly and democratically competitive, have faced no repression from any quarters. The spate of continued bombings and Tupamaro attention to Che Guevara raises questions about the demise of seeking power by terrorist means for the group.

Analogous concerns have been raised for various other developed-country groups—Baader-Meinhoff; the Red Brigades and Armies in Italy, Turkey, and Japan; Direct Action—and various spinoffs in the past and present. A second generation of terrorists has emerged in western Europe, with considerable drawing power among women in their late twenties who seem to be well-enough educated linguistically to move across state boundaries easily. On the surface the groups appear to be far-left Marxist-Leninist in their leanings, but their manifestos are incoherent, even while their methods are efficient and uncompromising.[16]

Terror as Fad

A close corollary behavior pattern of the nonpolitical power-seeking terrorist is terror as fad. Faddism is a common phenomenon among segments of an affluent society in both developed and underdeveloped countries. Young people in their most impressionable periods (high school and university years) are often taken with causes. The setting permits a most idealistic, purist orientation because of the freedom from specific obligations and commitments to the social system, which usually come later.

Casuistry has an ongoing dynamic of its own that can easily sustain itself during this youthful period and continue for the affluent into the socioeconomic order afterwards. The concept of *noblesse oblige* or philanthropic endeavor toward the less fortunate in society is well understood in western European and U.S. traditions. For most of the upper and middle classes a single cause may be sufficient involvement for the duration of their life, but the rarer few need to move from cause to cause, constantly seeking new challenges. Unless a new cause is discovered, novelty is missing, and boredom and disenchantment with the world may set in. In popular parlance, the need is for a constant source of "kicks." Enter into the picture the combination of a new need, a new cause, and a possible disillusionment with prior failed causes or a succession of them: it becomes all too simple to generalize a pattern of overall failure of the social system and opt for violence as an exciting activity in itself or as a means to some vaguely polemicized goal.

Examples of this phenomenon have been observed in the transition of some of the Students for a Democratic Society into the Weathermen Underground terrorist organization, after failing to woo automobile workers during the 1960s. A comparable development has occurred in western European and Latin American terrorist movements among both the affluent, intellectual left and right. Radical religious fundamentalist groups in U.S. society have evidenced the same tendency in their recruitment and commitment patterns, although many of their adherents come from the *nouveaux riches* since World War II, as opposed to the older elite that served as the spawning ground for left-oriented terrorists.

Potential or actual faddist terrorists usually evidence a cultist mentality or outlook. Common symbols are shared as validations of their correct choice and commitments. For example, Costa-Gavras's films have served over the years to confirm their attitudes and have been a source of mystique for such groups.[17] At the level of political psychological analysis, the faddist evidences what Richard Hofstadter and others have labelled "the paranoia syndrom," constant delusions of grandeur and persecution, often at the same time.[18]

Conclusion

Politically motivated forms of terrorism offer some prospects of either resolution or conflict management. Rational categories as commonly understood and perceived can produce rational responses. However, once irrational terrorism and its variations are recognized for what they are, optimism must give way to pessimism about dealing with the phenomena rationally. Personality problems cannot be resolved for everyone drawn to these kinds of behavior, (even assuming they are readily identifiable in the first place).

Furthermore, the social and physical settings of the "open" societies are much too conducive to irrational terrorism emerging as an alternative style of behavior. In open societies, and even "closed" ones (authoritarian and totalitarian societies are never completely closed), inequities, injustices, and discrepancies in status and lifestyles are known to the less fortunate, the impacted, or the guilt-ridden causists. Some will choose to react by violent means. This cannot be prevented. Also, open societies pride themselves on the freedom of movement that is vital to the very nature of such a system but is simultaneously a facilitator of terrorist activities. Once the critical judgement is made, therefore, that causal or conditional factors associated with irrational terrorism can neither be preempted or prevented, the best that is achievable is to maximize the damage control efforts applicable to other forms of terrorism—cooperation, intelligence gathering, surveillance, counterpropaganda, and counterforce. At best, the prospects are for the management of terrorism as opposed to the resolution of it.

Notes

1. Conor Cruise O'Brien, "Thinking About Terrorism," *Atlantic*, No. 257 (1986), 62–66.
2. Simcha Jacobovici, "The Ideology of Terror," *Middle East Focus*, Vol. 4, No. 3 (September 1981), 14; Charles Waterman, *Christian Science Monitor*, 3 December 1986, p. 14.
3. Richard Hofstadter, *Anti-Intellectualism in American Life* (New York: Alfred A. Knopf, 1969), Chapter 15; Seymour Lipset and Earl Raab, *Politics of Unreason* (New York: Harper & Row, 1970), Chapters 1, 11, and 12; Paul Wilkinson, *Terrorism and the Liberal State* (New York: New York University Press, 1986), Chapters 3 and 5.
4. Bernard Schechterman, *Religious Fanaticism as a Cause of Political Violence* (Coral Gables, Florida: International Freedom Foundation, 1985), Monograph No. 3.
5. Jacobovici, p. 13.
6. *Ibid*.
7. *Ibid*.; Wilkinson, pp. 72–77 and 96–98.
8. Jacobovici, p. 13; Wilkinson, pp. 99–100.
9. Robin Wright, "A New Generation of Antagonists," *Christian Science Monitor*, 7 November 1986, pp. 9, 10.
10. *Ibid*.
11. Robin Wright, "Free Lance Terrorism Undercuts Syria," *Christian Science Monitor*, 6 November 1986, 1, 14.
12. *Ibid*.; David Horovitz, "How Syrian Ties with Terrorism Were Exposed," *Jerusalem Post*, 8 November 1986, pp. 1, 2; Yoram-Ettan-Ettinger, "Root Cause of International Terrorism," *Houston Post*, 19 September 1986, p. 3B.
13. Richard Hofstadter, pp. 416–432; Lipset, pp. 513–514.
14. Bernard Schechterman, "Shi'ite [*sic*] Power Plays Color Crisis," *Miami News*, 28 June 1985, Op-Ed Page.
15. Shirley Christian, "Surviving Tupamaros of Uruguay," *New York Times*, 3 November 1986, Section A.
16. *Miami Herald*, "Second Generation Killers . . . ," 27 November 1986, p. 1G.
17. Jacobovici, p. 14.
18. Hofstadter, pp. 416–432.

Part 2

Some Dimensions of Terrorism

Counterterrorism

4

JOSEPH RICHARD GOLDMAN

The phenomenon of terrorism -international and national- is increasingly an important part of security studies at military service schools in the United States and abroad. The American war colleges today have courses taught by civilian and military experts for students who someday might be generals or admirals but now must have more knowledge about terrorism and its relationship to national security. Of some significance are at least two policy questions concerned with terrorism and security management: What policy tools are being applied effectively in managing terrorism? and, Given some basic understandings about terrorist phenomena, what lessons are useful toward contributing to American and Western security? These questions (and many others, of course) about terrorism are both academic and policy oriented in the schools which prepare military officers who will have assignments that could expose them to this type of political behavior. What American (and friendly - i.e., Allied and nonaligned) military officers know about terrorism and its associated phenomena of political violence is a relatively underdeveloped area of inquiry. When one considers the growing importance of US military assistance to many Third World friends in the form of knowledge involving all sorts of security problems, we should know more now about military education and its relationship to terrorism.

Consequently, this discussion will confine itself specifically to what aspects of terrorism is taught at the service schools, and to some prescriptions proffered to control terrorism (note, not necessarily "remedy" terrorism since that phenomenon requires long-lasting political rather than purely military treatment). While military specialists of terrorism are equally interested in theories of terrorism, they must concentrate their efforts on having instruments for controlling terrorism besides scrutinizing its associated properties stemming from human behavior.

To begin with, there are many aspects of terrorism which can engage military policy makers' and advisers' interest. For our purposes, let us establish a simple pattern that includes the most important aspects of terrorism for military involvement.

By no means should this pattern be construed to mask the complexities of terrorism; rather it is a parsimonious representation of the basic types that terrorism assumes from a security point of view. The historical, psychological, and strategic factors surrounding the acts of political terrorism are half of the equation studies by the military (and taught to their pupils in security assistance programs); while the operational (diplomatic, economic, and military) elements comprise the other half of this equation (and equally taught to their pupils in security assistance programs). When the four types of terrorism are examined by these six factors involved in terrorism, one can see which direction this equation is emphasized more: the operational if we accept the notion that the military is a component of any

FIGURE 1
Some Basic Types of Terrorism

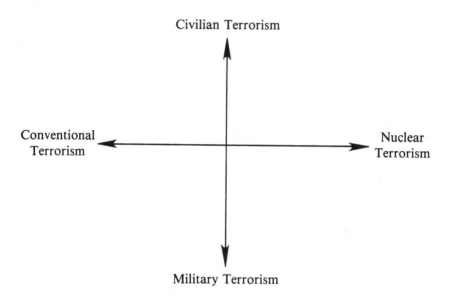

Civilian Terrorism

Conventional Terrorism

Nuclear Terrorism

Military Terrorism

political management regarding terrorism.

Security assistance means whatever advice, aid and activities the US military will proffer to designated recipients (domestic and foreign) under any guidelines imposed by some agency of government under authority of the President or his recognized deputies. Highly trained individuals (managers and executors) in terrorist problems include people from combat arms specialties, military intelligence and the military police. They are the products of Training and Doctrine Command and Force Command centers in this country, and their Allied or non-aligned (but friendly) counterparts overseas might be graduates of Fort Leavenworth and Fort Bragg.

We mentioned earlier four broad types of terrorism (civilian terrorism; military terrorism; conventional terrorism; nuclear terrorism) that concern the military. Each category contains within it diverse forms, and any category can be affected by "spillover" from another. For simplicity's sake, each type of terrorism will be discussed in terms of issues and concerns, and where possible linked with others when spillover effects might occur. Empirical evidence will be put forward in terms of actual cases or examples to move from the realm of hypothetical to practical as the situation in question permits.

Civilian Terrorism. Terrorism aimed at civilian personnel has often times been in the news. The 1972 Munich massacre of Israeli athletes by the "Black September" offshoot of Fatah, or the 1986 Rome-Vienna killings of travellers by suicide assassins belonging to Abu Nidal's faction of the PLO are but two examples of international terrorism really aimed at destroying the State of Israel politically. Europe and the Middle East are not the only theaters of violence. American nuns in El Salvador a few years ago were killed by right-wing terrorists some of whom used soldiers in the Army as triggermen. At times terrorism is directed at national figures who are political, religious or economic notables to achieve a psychological effect that terrorists want on their real target - the public. The IRA's attempt on Prime Minister Margaret Thatcher of Great Britain in 1984, or M 19's destruction of the Colombian Supreme Court justices in 1985 are two examples.

While such acts of civilian terrorism are international from the American viewpoint (but domestic from that nation's public when occurring), urban and rural terrorism from MOVE or the Order do concern military security specialists here. Of course, the FBI and local police ostensibly handle radical groups which use violence as a political means of expression. The US military however has access to FBI reports, and stores any information away for later use in studying possible case scenarios of urban and rural terrorism which military advisers may come into contact later.

Studies of terrorism naturally focus on insurgency operations and how to counter them. The terrorist organizations which specifically attack civilians as bystanders or targets are examined in terms of psychology, history and strategy. Knowing the ecology surrounding terrorism and terrorist organizations is the key to these studies by military experts in security assistance. Lessons derived from post behavior sometimes become rules and procedures codified in some field manual or briefing given to students. Whole psychological operations campaigns are devised by military and civilian specialists to deal with terrorism particularly in neutralizing the effects of terrorism (fear) on its real victims - a target population. Although these psychological operations campaigns can be defensive, they also have offensive capabilities too. Operation Phoenix in Vietnam and some Contra programs in Nicaragua today fall into this category.

Military Terrorism. Military terrorism involves professionally trained soldiers and amateur guerrilla fighters who apply terrorism to retain a regime's power or seize it. That is another aspect of insurgency - counterinsurgency terrorist theory; however, it is not the only one. The killing of 243 US Marines in Beirut during 1983 by a faction (or factions) using a suicide bomber driving a truck laden with explosives into the Marine barracks near the airport is one tragic example of military terrorism. The selective mutilation and killing of military prisoners in the early stages of the Soviet-Afghan war on both sides is another case in point. Both serve to teach that war is in the mind of its beholder; killing the symbols of oppression or resistance in order to dissuade others is terrorism too. Many low intensity conflicts (LICS) in the Third World are susceptible to acts of military terrorism, and some regimes employ this type as another instrument of politics. Military terrorism is also possible when a coup brings a new leadership to power and the army is sent to the streets to cow civilian opponents and bystanders alike (as in the 1985 coup in Monrovia, Liberia). Finally, military terrorism exists when forces of a country at war with another use deliberate and needless

35

political violence against the enemy civilian populace such as the present Iran-Iraq war exhibits along their mutual borders, or Vietnam-Cambodia since 1978.

Conventional Terrorism. All of the above examples spill over into this category, plus more. But another distinction must be made about conventional terrorism, and that is in regards to weaponry more than anything else. In every case of terrorism until now, conventional weapons are the means of inflicting suffering, maiming and death. Guns, grenades, explosives are some of the weapons used by terrorists on their victims. (Nuclear weapons will be discussed as separate category.) Terrorist organizations themselves are "conventional" in terms of membership and leadership (unless a terrorist operates as an "organization of one" when phoning the media to take credit or announce a threat concerning terrorism). Terrorist groups may be transnational organizations like the Palestine Liberation Organization, or domestic such as "Shining Path" in Peru. They may be outlawed in two countries as the IRA is in Great Britain and Ireland, or state-supported like Uruguay and Argentina until the mid 1980's when democratic governments put an end to these units at least for the time being. And this list could go on about terrorist strategies and tactics against governments, corporations or private individuals and groups terrorism seeks to harm. In all, terrorism is war by the few against another few in the midst of a many in the way. It can be systematic or sporadic, and always difficult to control - much less eradicate. Here intelligence is critical for saving lives and property (counterterrorism), or taking them (terrorism); the lessons and principles drawn from conventional terrorism are important to those applying political violence for specific purposes.

Nuclear Terrorism. This is a phenomenon whose appearance is yet to be made. Dramatizations such as *Special Bulletin* (1983) where terrorists fashion a nuclear weapon that eventually obliterates Charleston, South Carolina may be science fiction, but they are plausible and well within the realm of probability. Since the proliferation of nuclear technology abroad by the United States and the Soviet Union first during the 1950's, the numbers of nuclear states possessing weapons or convertible technology has grown substantially by the 1980's. It is no secret that Khaddafy of Libya wanted to buy or develop a nuclear weapon from any country (or countries) willing to assist him. The possibility of local terrorist groups stealing a nuclear weapon from an American installation in the United States may seem remote, it might be less so in countries where US warheads are stored in Europe and Asia. Again, the possibility exists although the probability is for now extremely low.

But nuclear terrorism is not only a bomb in unauthorized and dangerous hands. This type of terrorism can make a nuclear power plant into a radiological weapon. In every nation where nuclear reactors exist to make electricity, the potential for terrorism is there. Plant security is usually a civil matter in peace time, and the record so far is possibility "n," actuality "o." Only so far, however. Nor does nuclear terrorism require weaponry in the megatonnage or kilotonnage scale to be convincing. Scenarios by

36

government agencies in the United States and other nuclear countries abound where terrorists somehow possess very small and dirty nuclear devices which can be placed and detonated anywhere in a target state. Any conveyance might be of use other than a missile; as *Special Bulletin* aptly showed, a tugboat can work. The prospect of nuclear terrorism coexisting with all other types of terrorism mentioned here is certainly appalling to many people, appealing to a few.

This essay sought to open another area of inquiry dealing with terrorism and national security. The role of the military to terrorism is not new, nor are the questions of the uses of military power to affect terrorism (or vice-versa) necessarily novel. But the role of terrorism to security studies ought not be surprising. Just as terrorism is a field of inquiry for universities and think tanks in America and elsewhere, so has it become for the war colleges particularly in recent times (just as the Vietnam war and the Middle East were stimuli for American military interest; the violent decolonization experiences for the British, French, Dutch and Portuguese after World War II accomplished the same interest; and terrorism always was of interest to the Soviet bloc in terms of its tactical usefulness than threat potential to bloc interests or survival).

The basic typology put forward is by no means a precursor to another formal model (it could be, naturally) as much as it serves as a teaching device upon which more elaborate research is encouraged. The four types of terrorism (civilian terrorism; military terrorism; conventional terrorism; nuclear terrorism) are security problems which do engage military interest. Three of these basic types occur in many ways at different places. The literature in books and journals on them is extensive and empirically valid. The nuclear terrorism type is, on the other hand, somewhat new and developing - but with problems affecting (afflicting?) this development. Much information is highly classified. Publishing data about nuclear devices and weapons also spreads information to those elements who might employ this knowledge to terrorism somehow. Reportage of incidents where sabotage really existed at a nuclear installation is not always available nor reliable. Despite these obstacles - both governmental and commercial - research on nuclear terrorism is continuing. Security studies has an advantage now where it is conducted by specialists at the war colleges: these researchers have access to classified information others in universities would like to have and cannot. Be that as it may, the problem of nuclear terrorism is a serious one which goes beyond classroom exercises or war games.

The phenomenon of terrorism is an important area that will absorb more energy and effort by those in security studies. As their research comes into the disciplines of history and political science, for example, the continuing exchange of ideas and information among the service schools and their university and think tank counterparts will contribute to our understanding of terrorism. In the meantime, terrorism will be an important factor in security studies and for those nations needing knowledge to manage this danger for their well-being.

The State as Terrorist

MARTIN SLANN

Various social sciences have sought to identify and characterize the psychology, ideology, and goals of political movements using terrorist activities. Usually, those activities seek to undermine and discredit a society's governing process by making millions of individuals aware that, even as political innocents, they are vulnerable to violence. What is often unclear or overlooked is that the government itself may be utilizing violence, at least partially, to achieve its goals. As John McCamant has put it, "One searches in vain through the thousands of articles and books written by political scientists, political sociologists, economists, and anthropologists for references to the awful and bloody deeds of governments and for explanations of how and why these deeds are done."[1] This chapter attempts to illuminate the more brutal and sustained features of state terrorism.

Characteristics of State Terrorism

The most notorious historical examples of state terrorism—Stalin's purges in the 1930s and the Nazi regime's atrocities (1933–1945)—are especially frightening because they are so recent and because they were among the most lethal: coercion by the state was unchecked even by the usual norms of common sense and political prudence.[2] In these, as in numerous other instances, terror became so politically useful it seemed to develop a reckless permanency of its own.[3] State terrorism becomes institutionalized when this occurs.

Even though, predictably, terrorist organizations have often referred to the governments they oppose as "terrorist"—for example, the IRA in Northern Ireland and the Basque ETA in Spain consider their targets to be aggressors and occupiers of an exploited nation—for the purposes of this essay, however, an acceptable definition of state terror is "the more precise and deliberate act of inflicting harm on an individual or group in order to change the nature of their behavior and/or instill fear in other individuals or groups."[4]

This definition was first applied to South Africa, and for good reason. The psychological dimensions of the South African government's apartheid policies are obvious and have been most pronounced in the country's educational system, where the African school-age population is made aware in numerous ways year after year of its inferior social and political position. Certainly, the government prefers this form of "psychological terrorism" to more violent forms of pressure. State terrorism, then, does not always manifest as physical violence, although the threat is always present. This is an advantage that terrorists operating without government sanction conspicuously lack.

The state as terrorist is not a new concept or phenomenon. Anarchists (who often take on the appearance of terrorists themselves) have argued for centuries that the state, in any form, is an unmitigated and unnatural evil; and that physically and psychologically, it is an intimidating apparatus capable of any outrage.[5] The anarchists' message, however, is difficult to publicize, in part because the state

39

most often controls the communications network. After all, "when state terrorism surfaces the government is usually quick in censoring the media. The net effect is an imbalance in the news coverage of terrorism. Informed only by the mass media, the average news consumer gets the impression of a unilateral upsurge in mainly left-wing insurgent terrorism,"[6] even though state terrorism is both more pronounced and more effective.

The state obviously has great potential to do harm. This is especially true if a government has at its disposal the tremendous resources offered by modern communication and transportation systems, which it usually does. The state ultimately controls or at least monitors extensively the exchange of information at all levels of society. Antistate terrorists have long appreciated this fact and have imitated the state's use of ruthless example to intimidate.[7] When a crowded marketplace is blown up or a plane hijacked, millions of people know about it within minutes. However, they are only temporarily horrified and intimidated; that is all any terrorist organization, even the most resourceful and well funded, can hope to accomplish. The apparatus of the state, however, can perpetuate continuing, relentless intimidation because of its maximum and often monopolized resources.

Certain forms of state terrorism actually enjoy a genuinely popular base. Iranian enthusiasm over the seizure of U.S. diplomatic personnel in 1979 is a case in point. When the hostages were seized, the students who took over the U.S. Embassy compound had only the most tenuous connection with the government. When the revolutionary regime realized the popular support for the act, it quickly condoned and eventually completely dominated the proceedings. The original act became an activity of state terrorism with widespread domestic support.[8]

A terrorist government can also seek to increase its influence abroad or sustain its effectiveness at home by exporting its version of revolutionary justice. In October 1986, for example, the Syrian Embassy in London became a virtual base for a terrorist effort to blow up an El Al flight. And less than two years earlier, the British had ordered the Libyan Embassy closed when a member of the embassy's staff (with full diplomatic immunity) shot and killed a British police officer. This transforming of a diplomatic headquarters into a terrorist enclave, which has become known as the "terrorist embassy,"[9] is almost without precedent in international relations. Embassies of rival states include spies on their staffs and even secret police detachments; however, even the tactics of Germany's embassies under the Nazis were more subtle and less violent than those of the terrorist state today. The Western political democracies, in particular, are now seeing in effect an outpost of the terrorist state established within their own capital cities. Using such means to extend its influence and presence, the terrorist state perpetuates its power and programs.

State terrorism is typically perceived by its perpetrators to be justified. "Government violence and even unjust violent policies are exempt from a definition of terrorism as long as we accord a legitimate monopoly of violence to the state and its duly authorized functionaries."[10] In other words, governments can get away with more violence than can any other institution in society, because of unrivaled resources, and because there is usually either some popular support for even the most brutal political regime or legitimization of the government from outside by the recognition of international law.

40

Gradations of State Terrorism

There are, of course, gradations of state terrorism, ranging from bad to worse. These are summarized below:

1. Intimidation—government attempts to anticipate and discourage dissent and opposition. Current noteworthy examples include Chile and South Africa, where intimidation occurs usually through control of the media and the widespread presence of police.
2. Coerced conversion—government seeks a complete overhaul of a national life-style, usually following a revolution. Nicaragua and Iran are obvious examples.
3. Selective genocide or autogenocide—government seeks to eliminate physically an entire class, ethnic or religious group, or other minority for ideological reasons. Two of the most pronounced examples are the Stalinist purge of the Ukrainian kulaks and the Nazi-perpetrated annihilation of European Jewry.

Obviously, there can be and often is some overlap among these categories. There is, for example, the charge that the Sandinistas of Nicaragua are pursuing a determined policy of near genocide against the Miskito Indians even as they attempt to indoctrinate the remainder of the population in Marxist ideology. And certainly the Nazi regime engaged in all three gradations of state terror.

Intimidation is almost universally used by terrorist governments. Conversion, on the other hand, appeals to those regimes that seek a profound change in a population's social and political environment. When conversion is coerced, of course, its effects can be brutal and even lethal. At least, though, conversion to a political or religious doctrine allows physical survival, which cannot be said of genocide. Here conversion is not considered a viable alternative. This most extreme form of state terrorism offers victims no hope at all of survival. When physical elimination of an entire community is the avowed purpose of a regime, the terror state can pursue the policy methodically and without interruption and usually without opposition. Moreover, a compelling ideology or charismatic leadership can be so persuasive that genocide assumes for its perpetrators a noble and even historically inevitable act.

A most lethal derivation of selective genocide is autogenocide, where the government is intent on destroying a large portion of its own citizenry. A recent example is Cambodia between 1975 and 1979, when the Pol Pot regime brutalized and starved between one and two million of the country's seven million inhabitants.[11] Had the regime endured, it is unlikely that any element of the population would have been able to oppose it.

Variants of State Terrorism

Once in power, a regime can indulge in a variety of terrorist enterprises. Besides settling old scores within the state, a regime can, as we have seen, export terror to foreign enemies and can also visit revenge on dissidents who have gone into exile. Examples of state sponsorship of terrorism are suggested in Table 1.

Obviously, state terrorism can become undifferentiated from the sporadic activities of terrorists' groups not aligned with the state. This is certainly the case in the second and third categories given in Table 1. In the first category, however,

41

TABLE 1
State Terrorism

Type	Description	Example
State-directed	Reign of terror	French Revolution, 1792-1794; Iran, early 1980s
State-tolerated	Private death squad	El Salvador and Guatemala, 1970s
State-exported	Selective assassination	Trotsky's murder in Mexico, 1940; Qaddafi exiles abroad

state involvement is immediate and direct. And all three types illustrate the fact that state terrorism is capable of assuming any sort of ideological posture, whether of the extreme right or left or of religious fundamentalism.[12]

Primitivism and Zealotry

In some instances the terrorist state's goal is in essence to return to a purer, more primitive situation from the past. Many terrorist regimes have expressed such a desire. They regard the present as decadent and corrupt, and their attempts to return to an idealized past, while awkward and occasionally suicidal, are sincere. Some terrorist states have been criticized by their own advocates for not being firm enough in this regard. Julius Evola, for example, considered Mussolini's Italy to be a step in the right direction, but not fully committed to restoring the pristine values of the pre–Christian Roman state.[13]

In the 1980s, religious zealotry has become the most familiar characteristic of terrorist movements. This new terrorism is marked also by increasingly overt state sponsorship. The combination is both effective and frightening. Peter Merkl has written that "religious fanaticism and ethnic prejudice apparently can make the more selective *brigatisi* [Italian terrorists] and Baader-Meinhof terrorists look relatively humane."[14] Given the spectacle of a fully equipped state apparatus supporting theologically inspired terrorist acts, this is not an understatement.

This fundamentalism has become the primary motivation of contemporary terrorist states and has profoundly influenced their foreign policies as well. There are frequent references to the United States, Israel, and the West in general as "satanic." The more pronounced features of these "purist" regimes may be summarized as:

1. Compelling ideological or theological message
2. Total intolerance of dissent
3. Antipathy toward normal interplay of democratic polities
4. Extremist harassment of political, ethnic, or religious minorities
5. State inseparable from, and the self-designated enforcer of, the "truth"
6. Perennial conflict with external foes
7. Frequent denigration of and lack of concern with standard of living

As irrational as these may seem from a western viewpoint, it is important to keep in mind that even the most extreme form of fanaticism has, for the terrorist state, its own rationale. Terrorists do not see themselves as irrational and neither do terrorist states. Sartre implied a disconcerting parallel when he questioned whether, as repulsive as Palestinian terrorism may be, the Israeli state's destructive power is any less so when visited on Palestinian refugee camps?[15] Governments that sponsor or indulge in acts of terrorism have consistently claimed that, at best, they are simply vanguards in the fight for freedom and human progress and, at worst, they are engaging in the historically respected option of retaliation.

Moreover, the terrorist state seeks to preserve itself and assume legitimacy by joining the world political community and participating in its exchanges. It does not directly declare war against its perceived enemies, because it is not equipped to do so. Instead, like Libya, Syria, or Iran, the terrorist state opts for a policy of constant harassment against its foes.

The rational agenda of a terrorist regime should not be misunderstood or underestimated. Such an agenda may be hostile to democratic concerns and values, but it is supposed to be. The Iranian government or Iranian-inspired fanatics in Lebanon kidnapping or killing journalists, diplomats, or scholars is considered to be a legitimate method of bringing attention to a particular issue or securing compliance with a demand. Fundamentalist-based terrorist governments, after all, invoke a "higher" law than the international code that most countries accept as binding. It should be remembered that "terrorist-supporting nations will not surrender seriously held ambitions to expand their power and influence simply because the law is against them. Legal argument alone will not protect lawabiding nations and peoples against Quaddafi or Iran's Khomeini."[16]

Conclusion

In essence, state terrorism challenges, as well as departs from, the Western tradition of political philosophy. Possibly the terrorist state is simply a new formulation of the old conflict between despotism and democracy; between the point of view that the state precedes and is superior to the individual and the classical concept of individual sovereignty.

There is also the complementary concern that the most notorious terrorist states are also those most inspired by an absolutist, usually religious-based ideology. Fanaticism, however, in any form has never been compatible with political democracy and has consistently been in relentless opposition to it. Thus, state terrorism, regardless of the ideological direction of the regime, is basically antithetical to a Western political tradition that disavows extremism and insists on constitutional government. As authoritarian regimes headed by political or religious zealots become more plentiful than democratic polities,[17] it is incumbent upon democratic societies to fully understand the myriad dimensions of all forms of state terror.

Notes

[1] John F. McCamant, "Governance Without Blood: Social Sciences's Antiseptic View of Rule; or, The Neglect of Political Repression," in Michael Stohl and George A. Lopez, eds., *The State as Terrorist: The Dynamics of Governmental Violence and Repression* (Westport, Connecticut: Greenwood Press, 1984), p. 11.

[2] Stalin's purges, for example, decimated hundreds of thousands of loyal and talented communists; the Holocaust that consumed both Jews and non-Jews used up substantial amounts of German personnel and materiel needed for Germany's war effort.

[3] It also developed a bureaucracy of its own, as suggested by the thousands of Nazi SS clerks who kept meticulous records on daily genocide.

[4] Robert A. Denmark and Howard P. Lehman, "South Africa: The Costs of Containing Repression," in Stohl and Lopez, *The State as Terrorist,* p. 184.

[5] However, before states developed, terrorism was practiced extensively in primitive societies by members of one clan against victims captured in conflict with another clan.

[6] Alex Peter Schmid and Janny de Graaf, *Violence as Communication: Insurgent Terrorism and the Western News Media* (Beverly Hills, California: Sage Publications, 1982), p. 85.

[7] For an example of this point, see Schmid and de Graaf, *Violence as Communication.*

[8] An excellent account of this unusual sort of terrorism is found in Warren Christopher, et al., *American Hostages in Iran: The Conduct of a Crisis* (New Haven and London: Yale University Press, 1985).

[9] See the commentary by Yoram-Eytan Ettinger, "Is There a Way to Find the Root Cause of International Terrorism?" *The Houston Post,* 19 September 1986, p. 3E.

[10] Peter H. Merkl, "Approaches to the Study of Political Violence," in Peter H. Merkl, ed., *Political Violence and Terror: Motifs and Motivations* (Berkeley, Los Angeles, London: University of California Press, 1986), p. 20.

[11] No one will ever be sure of the numbers. Some good guesses are made by Elizabeth Becker, *When the War Was Over: The Voices of Cambodia's Revolution and Its People* (New York: Simon and Schuster, 1986).

[12] Religious fundamentalism itself is capable of springing from a variety of religious persuasions. Most, if not all, religions have the unpleasant and often contradictory ability to inspire both fanaticism and violence. See, for example, David C. Rapoport, "Fear and Trembling: Terrorism in Three Religious Traditions," *The American Political Science Review,* vol. 78, no. 3 (September 1983), pp. 658–676, and Bernard Schechterman, "Religious Fanaticism as a Factor in Political Violence" (Coral Gables, Florida: The International Freedom Foundation, 1984).

[13] See Richard H. Drake, "Julius Evola and the Ideological Origins of the Radical Right in Contemporary Italy," in Merkl, *Political Violence and Terror: Motifs and Motivations,* pp. 61–89. Evola even traced the decline of the West from pagan times, where free inquiry helped to undermine traditional values and belief systems.

[14] Peter H. Merkl, "Conclusion: Collective Purposes and Individual Motives," in Merkl, *Political Violence and Terror,* p. 361.

[15] For a discussion of how confusing the sources of terrorism are see, Haim Gordon, *Dance, Dialogue, and Despair: Existentialist Philosophy and Education for Peace in Israel* (University, Alabama: University of Alabama Press, 1986).

[16] Abraham D. Soafer, "Terrorism and the Law," *Foreign Affairs,* vol. 64, no. 5 (Summer 1986), p. 922.

[17] See, for example, Juan J. Linz, *The Breakdown of Democratic Regimes: Crisis, Breakdown, and Equilibrium* (Baltimore, Maryland: The Johns Hopkins Press, 1986).

Rhetoric and Values in Terrorism

6

RICHARD W. LEEMAN

> Howard Metzenbaum (on WKYC-TV, Cleveland):
> "If he's (Qaddafi) a party to killing innocent
> Americans, innocent people from all over the world,
> without any compunction whatsoever, then why need
> we have such compunction about seeing to it that he
> personally---"
> Mr. Feagler: "---So we assassinate him?"
> Senator Metzenbaum: "It would not be the first
> time."[1]

In this essay I wish to explore why a liberal U.S. senator such as
Metzenbaum would make a statement like the one above—and why the
American public not only accepts but *expects* such rhetoric. I use
"rhetoric" purposefully, for I will argue that by understanding terrorism as
rhetoric, Metzenbaum's rhetoric in response can best be explicated.

Before beginning, however, I must include the standard disclaimer
necessary for analyzing terrorism. As Walter Laqueur writes, "No definition of terrorism can possibly cover all the varieties of terrorism that have
appeared throughout history."[2] Because terrorism has no firm definition,
generalizations are difficult if not impossible. In this essay, I will not attempt to generalize for all terrorism. Rather, I wish to locate in the act of
terrorism a rhetorical feature which is *often* present; namely, the epideictic
function of rhetoric. I will not, and cannot, argue that the epideictic function is always featured, nor can I argue that it is always or even usually the
predominant feature. What I do argue is that this epideictic feature of terrorism can be critical for perceiving the full meaning of the terroristic act;
and that failure to consider it may contribute to the difficulties of
understanding terrorism. Perhaps of greater importance, rhetoric which
arises in response to terrorism often does so with an understanding of terrorism as epideictic.

Terrorism as Epideictic Rhetoric

Aristotle divided rhetoric into three genres: forensic (judicial),
deliberative (political), and epideictic (ceremonial).[3] (1358a-1359b) Typically, scholars treat terrorism as deliberative rhetoric. For example, Michael
Stohl in *The Politics of Terrorism* argues that terrorism has four major purposes: to seek publicity (agenda-setting), to coerce bargaining, to force obe-
dience in the population, and/or to provoke authorities into repressive
measures. Although he suggests that other purposes exist, these four are the
major purposes, and Stohl's list is characteristic of current thought.[4] Other
purposes have been suggested, of course: psychological desire for violence,
sociological frustration, criminal desire for money, etc; and the literature is
replete with examples supporting each of these various "motivations for

terrorism." That terrorism can function as epideictic, however, receives only cursory attention.[5] Yet consideration of terrorism as epideictic is critical to understanding responses to it such as Metzenbaum's.

Epideictic is often written off as simply "ceremonial" rhetoric; recent scholars, however, have recognized epideictic as significant because it acts as reinforcement for existing values. By praising some values and condemning others, epideictic discourse works to "increase the intensity of adherence to values held in common by the audience and the speaker."[6] Thus, an epideictic speech does not simply 'decorate the occasion;' epideictic rhetoric is a confirming rhetoric which certifies the correctness of one's value hierarchy.

To understand terrorism as epideictic, terrorism must be considered as *response*. Terrorism as response simply recognizes that rhetoric does not occur in a vacuum. Rhetoric is more dialogue than monologue: it arises within and in response to existing discourse and the patterns of that discourse. For example, terrorism can function as epideictic rhetoric because the act or threat of violence directly contravenes the "system," or "establishment." No matter whether the "system" is democratic or not, violence is antithetical to the "order," because violence is disorderly. To use violence argues implicitly that the system is bad and, therefore, that values contrary to the system are good. This feature of violence extends beyond reaction to government, however. Violence is also antithetical to communication; i.e., when humans agree to communicate they imply to the other a respect for their person. To use violence is essentially to dehumanize one's victim, because communication is an essentially human characteristic.[7] When terrorists threaten or use violence, they imply an epideictic rhetoric; viz, that their values are correct; the system's, wrong.

The idea of actions arguing values is not new. Bowers and Ochs, for example, divide disputants into two groups: horizontal and vertical deviants. Horizontal deviants are those who agree with their opponents on basic issues; their differences are ones of degree. Vertical deviants are those that disagree fundamentally, and they are the rhetors most likely to move towards obscene actions (e.g., flag desecration) or violence (token or terroristic).[8]

Although terrorism does not always act as epideictic, what is striking about the phenomenon is how often the terrorist argues for the total destruction of the "system." A kind of balancing occurs: the means are extreme, so the ends are extreme also. Nechaev argued for the "prompt destruction of this filthy order."[9] Bakunin thought that the robber was society's "enemy *par excellence,*" for the robber had rejected society out of hand.[10] For the Tupamaros in Uruguay, "their primary objective, they say, is to discredit and destroy the political and economic system."[11] Ulrike Meinhof argued that the Baader-Meinhof group wanted to "hit the system in the face, to mobilize the masses, and to maintain international solidarity."[12] Of these two avowed purposes, the first and last are rhetorically epideictic; only the second functions as deliberative.

46

Students of terrorism frequently note that terrorists either seek to destroy the "system," or at least justify their violence by claiming to desire such destruction. Pridham notes that terrorism often involves a "fundamental rejection;" of recent left-wing groups Laqueur writes "they were certainly radical in the sense that they opposed 'the system,' the 'establishment,' that they wanted violent change."[13] Implicitly acknowledging violence as epideictic, Lodge writes that terrorists "neither use nor respect accepted channels of communication with the authorities...they contest the legitimacy of the state's authorities."[14]

Terrorism, however, does not simply delegitimize the "system." By denying another's values—through violent actions—the terrorist simultaneously confirms his or her own values. Such confirmation is precisely the function of epideictic rhetoric. Unless terrorism can be seen as epideictic, how does one explain Japanese Red Army hijackers using samuri swords?[15] Or that an Israeli counter-terrorist group called itself the "Wrath of God?" Fanon wrote in *The Wretched of the Earth* that Algerian terrorism against the French would "restore self-respect," and Patrick Pearse justified Irish terrorism arguing that "Blood is a cleansing and sanctifying thing."[16] Suicide terrorists use the 'ultimate sacrifice' to demonstrate their commitment to particular values.

David Rapoport, studying the Indian Thugs, Moslem Assassins and Jewish Sicarii, writes that "the holy terrorist believes that only a transcendent purpose which fulfills the meaning of the universe can justify terror."[17] However, Rapoport argues that modern terrorism can be "ordered rationally," that it is designed for "various domestic and international audiences," i.e., it is *deliberative* rhetoric.[18] Consequently, in Rapoport's view holy terrorism differs significantly from modern terrorism. Although modern terrorism does not generally spring from a religious tradition, I would argue that it frequently has a 'religious' quality about it because it can function as epideictic. That is, the terroristic act may not be affirming religious values, as in the tradition of the *fedayeen,* but it *is* affirming the values of the terrorist, even if these values are largely of a negative, anti-statist variety. The negative act of violence confirms positively one's values and one's commitment to those values.

Rapoport suggests that "the very idea of the holy entails contrast with the profane, the normal, or the natural."[19] Terroristic violence negates the profane order of affairs, normal daily living, our natural means of communication. In the process it confirms its own "holiness." Thus, Laqueur notes that although various groups of anarchists were "confirmed atheists...their belief in their cause had a deeply religious quality."[20] Nor does terroristic violence necessarily oppose a state in order to gain epideictic meaning; the act of violence carries with it a quality of confirmation because of its relationship to communication. For example, Laqueur writes that "the SS too held to a perverse idealism, a belief that only they *took values seriously.*"[21] America is not immune to such epideictic rhetoric. Regarding the bombing of abortion clinics, a Ku Klux Klan editor writes

"God Bless" those courageous young White Christians accused of the bombings. *They* are doing God's work, while other *so-called Christians set back in their pews like cowardly sheep* and refuse to even utter a whisper of protest.[22]

Scholars often write that terrorism is ineffective.[23] Yet they make such judgements from a point of view which regards terrorism as deliberative rhetoric; i.e., terrorism as a means towards effecting political change. Such a judgement is certainly a valid one to make, but it ignores terrorism as epideictic. However, terrorism has about it some distinctly non-deliberative qualities. For example, terrorism is generally a futile endeavor, yet it is on the rise.[24] Interestingly, Aristotle pointed out that epideictic rhetoric often praises that which is inexpedient. When holding a value becomes pragmatically costly, keeping that value becomes confirmation of its worth.[25] (1359a)

Successful terrorism also serves as confirmation of terrorism's epideictic potential. Several scholars note that terrorism is most successful when it works to rally an indigenous population against an outsider.[26] Partly this success is due to logistical reasons: colonial powers can be convinced to 'cut their losses,' terrorists can work more easily from a supportive native countryside, etc. Partly, however, the epideictic feature of terrorism works well in such an environment; as Horowitz notes, the PLO derives its strength from "its ability to reinforce and undergird organized opposition to Israel...not (from any ability to) inflict a mortal blow on its opponent."[27] The ends of epideictic are to 'undergird' and 'reinforce' a system of values; epideictic therefore 'undergirds' and 'reinforces' the group which shares those values. Terrorism does not have to function as an epideictic reinforcement of values, nor is the epideictic feature of 'terroristic discourse' necessarily the only motivation for such rhetoric. Frequently, however, epideictic rhetoric plays an important role in justifying terrorism, even if such justification is not the actual 'motivation' as such.

The Rhetoric of Response: Reflecting the Terror

Not only does rhetoric act in response, in fact it often mimics or reflects the rhetoric to which it responds. The "yes you are/no I'm not" discourse of children is an exemplar of such reflection. Piaget, studying the language of children, called this "primitive argument," but such rhetoric is not confined to children.[28] Even mature rhetors use reflective rhetoric, for it is a natural mode of argumentation. For example, Edelman writes that bureaucrats use bureaucratic jargon—even when disagreeing—in order to signal that the disagreement is 'in-house.' That is, the jargon demonstrates that the rhetor still holds the values of the group, in this case the bureaucracy.[29] The epideictic rhetoric of terrorism, and the various responses to such rhetoric, can profitably be viewed from the perspective of rhetoric as reflection.[30]

Terrorists themselves often perceive terrorism as reflective. The violence of their communication is a response to the violence of those they oppose. West German terrorists, for example, considered their acts as the proper response to the "structural violence" of the system.[31] The *Brigate Rosse* of Italy employed their terror to counter the "terror of the ruling class."[32] In 1972, three Japanese terrorists opened fire in Israel's Lod airport. Working in conjunction with the Popular Front for the Liberation of Palestine, the terrorists timed the raid to coincide with the fifth anniversary of the Six Day War. They named the terrorist team "The Squad of the Martyr Patrick Urguello," the hijacking partner of Leila Khaled who, unlike Khaled, had died in the foray. And if this was not "justification" enough for the violence, Israelis found this note:

> The raid launched today was a revolutionary *answer* to the Israeli massacre performed in cold blood by the butcher Moshe Dayan and his *devils* against the *martyr heroes* Ali Taha and Abdel Aziz Elatrash...This revolutionary *answer* was a *tribute* to the blood of two *heroes* who fell as a result of a cheap trick.[33]

Note that the violence is viewed as an appropriate response: it is an answer. Note, too, the language so characteristic of epideictic, or discourse of value: tribute, devils, heroes, martyrs. Terrorism is not only an affirmation of values; it is very often "justified" with claims that its violence is an appropriate negation of the violence of others.

Terrorism, then, frequently contains elements of epideictic, specifically an epideictic which condemns fundamentally the state, society, or whomever it opposes. It indicts its opposition, arguing that the terror employed is an appropriate response to the terror of the opposition. Because terrorism contravenes basic values, it is frequently viewed as a fundamental attack. When the Tupamaros killed kidnapped American Dan Mitrone in Uruguay, President Pacheco responded by labelling it "the greatest attack this country's political institutions have faced in this century."[34] Furlong is representative of scholarly opinion when he writes that "political terrorism is implicitly an attack on the authority of the state."[35]

Terrorism within a country is not always considered an attack on that country's values or system, however. Whose rhetoric the terrorism "responds to" is critical; i.e., whose rhetoric and values are being negated through the use of violence. France is an illustrative case. Cerny notes that, during the seventies, most terrorism in France was sporadic, not directed against the French nation. Consequently, the system was not threatened, and most calls by "hard-liners...fall on deaf ears." The "domestic brand of violence," however, by those such as the Breton Liberation Front, "arouses the political passions."[36]

The typical response to terrorism is illustrative of its epideictic nature as well as the persuasive use of reflective rhetoric. The epideictic nature of terrorism's attack on one's values justifies an extreme response to that rhetoric, and the violence inherent in terrorism suggests a reflective response of violence. Even a cursory survey of the literature on violence uncovers terrorism frequently countered by more terrorism. Scholars typically label this a "backlash," and the very metaphor of backlash suggests the reflective nature of such actions.[37] In Argentina the counter-terrorists ended up "mimicking the terrorists."[38] In Uruguay, letters from right wing organizations threatened to kill fifty Tupamaros for every foreigner killed.[39] Israel arrested Rabbi Meir Kahane for smuggling weapons following the Olympic massacre. He denied the allegation of arms smuggling, but he had argued that Israel should adopt the "terrorists' tactics."[40] That the two rhetorical domains can continue this reflection indefinitely is recognized in the phrase "cycle of violence," a phrase commonly employed both by the rhetors involved and the scholars observing from outside.[41] The literature on terrorism is filled with examples of public or state reaction to terrorism: the desire to retaliate, to respond in kind, to 'fight fire with fire.' In fact, one frequent aim of terrorism relies on this impulse: provocation. Guerillas such as Carlos Marighella urge their followers to violence with the argument that "the government has no alternative except to intensify repression."[42]

However, to argue that counter-terrorism has "no alternative" but to respond with violence is a misreading of reflective rhetoric. Rhetors *tend* to reflect the rhetoric to which they respond. In this case, those whose values are attacked by terrorism's epideictic rhetoric *tend* to respond with counter-violence. Such need not be the case. To begin, terrorism *can* be ignored, for it is not a life-threatening situation for most of the society or for the state.[43] As recently as November of 1985 a U.S. military intelligence officer said that terrorism is "another form of warfare. But terrorism is not a major policy problem. It's a policy nuisance."[44] Such a view finds terrorism less of a threat because the perspective is one of terrorism as warfare (i.e., instrumental), not terrorism as epideictic attack on one's values.

Even when terrorism is perceived as epideictic, it can be ignored or minimized. When the Tupamaros killed liaison to Uruguay Dan Mitrone, the Nixon Administration issued only a "White House Statement." The statement argued that "this callous murder emphasizes the essential inhumanity of the terrorists"—thus interpreting the murder as an epideictic affirming a value of inhumanity—but issued no calls for retaliation.[45] When the Lod airport massacre resulted in 25 killed and 72 wounded, including some Americans, Nixon released no statement, made no speeches, had no comments.

Ignoring terrorism as rhetoric is not the only alternative, however. Rhetors may, for example, choose to use the rhetoric of democracy or legality in response. Sometimes this may be used simply as a means of affirming one's own values; it says, essentially, that in contrast to terrorism's inhumanity, I shall remain civilized. That is, because such rhetoric so starkly highlights the values presented in terrorism, it similarly presents its own values in sharp relief. Such rhetoric typically talks of the 'civilized response,' the 'need to redouble diplomatic efforts,' and of 'combatting the problem within the *existing legal framework.*'

Rhetors may also employ democratic rhetoric in an effort to reformulate the geography of the discourse. They recast the discussion into democratic language hoping that the opposition will reflect that formula.[46]

The recent British-Irish pact on Northern Ireland is just such an attempt. The reaction to the pact, however, is not atypical. Reverend Ian Paisley called Thatcher a "quisling," and the Secretary of State for Northern Ireland was attacked by about fifty people shouting "traitor."[47] Such views are understandable, for the British have symbolically negated the values affirmed through violence by abandoning violence as a rhetorical tool. Of course, the situation is more complex than just epideictic symbolics: power, property, and lives are at stake, as well as mutual antipathy that makes any negotiation distasteful to some members of both sides. However, the symbolic importance of the British attempting to abandon violence (in the form of the Home Guard) in favor of the democratic language of diplomacy and negotiation ought not be underestimated.

Sometimes such non-reflective rhetoric does work. For example, Clutterback suggests the Geoffrey Jackson kidnapping as an illustrative case. Jackson, the British amabassador to Uruguay, was kidnapped and held by the Tupamaros for eight months. Communication between Jackson and his captors was at first tense, but Jackson's consistent use of gentle humor eventually broke through to his captors, and moved their relations to a more "human" level.[48] Such are the possibilities of using non-reflective rhetoric to fight fire not with more fire, but with water instead.

Conclusions

Terrorism has an epideictic feature inherent in its use of violence. Because violence is fundamentally antithetical to both the "system" and to human communication, it directs attention to the values which give rise to such violence. It also suggests implicitly that those values, like the violence, are antithetical to the values against whom the violence is directed. Marighella argued that urban guerilla violence in Brazil should be directed towards "the killing of a North American spy, of an agent of the dictatorship, of a police torturer, of a fascist personality in the government,...of a stool pigeon, informer, police agent, or police *provocateur.*"[49] The list suggests the values which Marighella would profess to hold, and those values he would disdain. Conversely, the Palestinian Zayed justified indiscriminate violence because there are no innocents, all are guilty if only because "they had not 'raised a finger for the Palestinians.'"[50] That list of victims clearly asserts his values.

Terrorism need not always be epideictic, nor is epideictic always the predominant feature of the discourse. Terrorists certainly have varied motivations, and they can mix those motivations in varying quantities. Genres of rhetoric, however, can also be mixed, and in varying degrees. Rhetoric can include forensic, epideictic and deliberative elements, or any two of the three. Further, a particular rhetor may decide to feature one genre over the other.[51]

However, terroristic violence *implies* an epideictic facet even if the terrorist does not mean it too. Thus, even if the violence is meant simply as a means to an end, e.g., to overthrow the government, the responding rhetor can plausibly read into the violence a rhetoric threatening the value system.

Further, because the threat is couched in symbol—the method of rhetoric—the lack of *physical* threat can be treated as immaterial. This symbolic challenge to the system makes coherent Reagan's justification for sanctions on Libya: because of "an unusual and extraordinary threat to the national security and foreign policy of the U.S."[52] Such a rhetorical response may not be accurate, but it is coherent given the epideictic challenge to our system.

Rhetors tend to reflect the rhetoric they oppose. Such is not necessarily the case, however. Whereas Nixon ignored the Lod airport massacre, Reagan has responded in a rather reflective manner. If the economic sanctions fail to stop Libya's assistance, "I promise you that further steps will be taken."[53] "Further steps," suggest that the economic violence of sanctions are likely to be followed by a less metaphorical, more literal violence.

Rhetoric is a dialogue. Rhetoric that "attacks," as terroristic violence does so both literally and symbolically, invites the rhetorical victim to respond. Because rhetors tend to reflect such an attack, the resulting impulse is to "counter-attack." Thus, a Senator Metzenbaum can justify violence against Qaddafi for two reasons: the violence of Rome and Vienna "demands" an answer, and Qaddafi's violence invites, indeed justifies, a violent answer. The ease with which rhetors employ such rhetorical dialogue is evident in George Shultz's challenge to the European states which chose to avoid the response of sanction:

> If you don't like what we're doing, what do you suggest be done? Personally, I don't think the answer can be nothing.[54]

Notes

[1]As reported in the *New York Times,* January 10, 1986, 7:1.

[2]Walter Laqueur, *Terrorism* (Boston: Little, Brown and Co., 1977), p. 7.

[3]Aristotle, *The Rhetoric and Poetics of Aristotle,* trans. W. Rhys Roberts (New York: The Modern Library, 1954), pp. 31-34.

[4]Michael Stohl, *The Politics of Terrorism,* 2nd ed. (New York: Marcel Dekker, 1983), pp. 3-5. For other examples, see Martha Crenshaw, *Terrorism, Legitimacy, and Power* (Middletown, Conn.: Wesleyan University Press, 1983), pp. 7-10; Laqueur, p. 109; and Richard Clutterback, *Living with Terrorism* (New Rochelle, N.Y.: Arlington House Publishers, 1975), p. 129.

[5]See J. Bowyer Bell, *Transnational Terrorism* (Washington, D.C.: American Enterprise Institute, 1975), pp. 16, 18; and Alex P. Schmid and Janny de Graaf, *Violence as Communication* (Beverly Hills: Sage, 1982).

[6]Chaim Perelman and L. Olbrechts-Tyteca, *The New Rhetoric,* trans. John Wilkinson and Purcell Weaver (Notre Dame: Notre Dame University Press, 1969), p. 52.

[7]See, for example, Dwight Van De Vate, Jr., "The Appeal to Force," and George Yoos, "A Critique of Van De Vate's 'The Appeal to Force,' *Philosophy and Rhetoric* 8 (1975), 43-60 and 172-176. Although the two authors have significant differences, both concur on the argument presented above.

[8]John Waite Bowers and Donovan J. Ochs, *The Rhetoric of Agitation and Control* (Reading, Mass.: Addison-Wesley, 1971), pp. 7-37. See also Herbert W. Simons, "Persuasion in Social Conflicts: A Critique of Prevailing Conceptions and a Framework for Future Research," *Communication Monographs* 39 (1972), 227-247; Robert L. Scott and Donald K. Smith, "The Rhetoric of Confrontation," *Quarterly Journal of Speech* 55 (1969), 1-8; and Richard J. Goodman and William I. Gorden, "The Rhetoric of Desecration," *Quarterly Journal of Speech* 57 (1971), 23-31. The latter specifically discusses desecration of the flag as an act which "negates the social order."

[9]S. Nechaev, *The Revolutionary Catechism,* in D.C. Rapoport, *Assassins and Terrorists* (Toronto: Canadian Broadcasting Corp, 1972), p. 71.

[10]Laqueur, p. 28.

[11]*New York Times,* 11 August 1970, p. 1:2.

[12]This is a paraphrase of court testimony, as reported in *The (London) Times*, 15 December 1972.

[13]Geoffrey Pridham, "Terrorism and the State of West Germany during the 1970s," in Juliet Lodge, ed., *Terrorism: A Challenge to the State* (N.Y.: St. Martin's Press, 1981), p. 22; and Laqueur, p. 176.

[14]Lodge, p. 226.

[15]*New York Times*, 31 March 1970, p. 1:3.

[16]Quoted in Laqueur, p. 206.

[17]David C. Rapoport, "Fear and Trembling: Terrorism in Three Religious Traditions," *American Political Science Review* 78 (1984), 658-677.

[18]Ibid, pp. 659, 674.

[19]Ibid, p. 674.

[20]Laqueur, p. 127.

[21]Laqueur, p. 75. Emphasis mine.

[22]*The Confederate Leader,* February 1985, p. 5. Emphasis mine.

[23]See, for example, Laqueur, pp. 117-118, 221; Crenshaw, pp. 26-27, Irving L. Horowitz "The Routinization of Terrorism and Its Unanticipated Consequences," in Crenshaw, p. 42; Clutterback, pp. 124, 131; and Paul Furlong, "Political Terrorism in Italy," in Lodge, p. 58.

[24]Horowitz, p. 39.

[25]Aristotle, p. 33.

[26]Laqueur, pp. 118, 223; Horowitz, pp. 45-46; and Clutterback, p. 124.

[27]Horowitz, ibid.

[28]Jean Piaget, *The Language and Thought of the Child,* trans. Marjorie and Ruth Gabain, 3rd ed. (London: Routledge and K. Paul, 1959), p. 66.

[29]Murray Edelman, *Politics as Symbolic Action* (Chicago: Markham Press, 1971), p. 74.

[30]For further discussion of rhetoric as reflective, see Richard W. Leeman, "Reflective Rhetoric: Its Framework and Utility in Explicating the Rhetoric of Prohibition and Repeal" (M.A. Thesis: University of Maryland, 1982).

[31]Pridham, p. 22.

[32]Furlong, p. 70-71.

[33]*New York Times*, 31 May 1972, p. 27:2. Emphasis mine.

[34]*New York Times*, 11 August 1970, p. 1:2.

[35]Furlong, p. 61. Of course, this is applicable only to anti-state terror.

[36]Philip G. Cerny, "France: Non-Terrorism and the Politics of Repressive Tolerance," in Lodge, p. 107.

[37]See, for example, Clutterback, p. 17; Crenshaw, pp. 10, 15, 16; Laqueur, p. 224; Lodge, p. 225, and Cerny, p. 92.

[38]Crenshaw, p. 140.

[39]*New York Times*, 10 August 1970, p. 1:2. Eventually right-wing militarists ousted the democratic government, using the terror of the Tupamaros as justification.

[40]*New York Times*, 2 October 1972, 10:4.

[41]For example of the former, see *New York Times*, 15 November 1985, 1:1 (concerning the recent British-Irish Pact) and 29 December 1985, p. 1:4 (following the Rome/Vienna airport massacres). For examples of the latter see Cerny, p. 111; and Crenshaw, p. 18.

[42]Carlos Marighella, *Minimanual of the Urban Guerilla,* reprinted in Robert Moss, *Urban Guerrilla Warfare* (London: International Institute for Strategic Studies, 1971), p. 40.

[43]See, for example, Bell, p. 88. Many scholars note the limited physical effect of terrorism's damage. See for example Horowitz, p. 45.

[44]*New York Times*, 26 November 1985, p. A10:1.

[45]*Weekly Compilation of Presidential Documents*, 10 August 1970.

[46]See, for example, Murray Edelman, *The Symbolic Uses of Politics* (Urbana: Univ. of Illinois Press: 1964), pp. 130-151.

[47]*New York Times*, 16 November 1985, p. 8:1 and 21 November 1985, p. 3:4.

[48]Clutterback, p. 135-136.

[49]Marighella, p. 34.

[50]*New York Times*, 4 June 1972, p. 10:1.

[51]Kathleen Hall Jamieson and Karlyn Kohrs Campbell, "Rhetorical Hybrids: Fusions of Generic Elements," *Quarterly Journal of Speech* 68 (1982), 146-157. I would also note that "genre" need not be restricted to the three divisions listed above.

[52]Executive Order 12543, 7 January 1986.

[53]*New York Times*, 8 January 1986, p. 1:6.

[54]*New York Times*, 16 January 1986, p. 8:1.

Part 3

Case Studies in Terrorism

Turkey and the Armenians

MICHAEL M. GUNTER

7

Contemporary Armenian terrorism against the Turks[1] has inevitably given rise to speculation concerning possible Turkish reprisals in the form of counterterror or harassment. The purpose of the following article is to analyze this situation.

Counterterror?—In 1983, the Turkish Foreign Minister Ilter Turkmen declared in an interview that: "it should be remembered that terror inevitably leads to counterterror."[2] After the bloody ASALA attack on the Ankara airport that summer and the murder of another Turkish diplomat in Canada, the Turkish President, Kenan Evren, bluntly declared: "The Turkish nation is patient. But there is a limit to patience... From now on, the Turkish state, the Turkish nation will feel free to take retaliatory measures."[3] Speaking immediately after the Orly bombing by ASALA in July 1983, Turkmen vowed: "The Turkish nation's retaliation will be as heavy as its patience has been great."[4] Still another report at that time stated "the situation may ultimately require Turkey's sending 'death squads' to pursue individual members of the Secret Army [ASALA]."[5] After a Turkish U.N. official, Enver Ergun, was assassinated by ARA on November 21, 1984, Salali Umer, a young Turkish doctor, was quoted as saying: "I have never had anything against Armenians before, but after the last attack, I met an Armenian in Cairo and I could scarcely control myself from—from doing something to him."[6]

Other reports, however, indicated that "Turkish officials—rather than planning a counterattack—admit to a 'fatalistic' attitude in regard to Armenian terrorism."[7] A Turkish diplomat about to go abroad, for example, declared: "Turks are generally not cowards, though they would be wiser if they were.... If they [assassins] can kill a President of the United States, they can kill anybody."[8] A Turkish news editor gave another reason why counterterror was not necessarily in the offering: "Our long history as a state and as an empire gives Turkey a psychological security.... We don't feel the need to hit back like the Israelis."[9] The same article in which this statement was carried added that Turkey "probably lacks the ability to carry out commando-style operations with the surgical accuracy of the Israelis."[10] In addition, "a highly informed" Turkish source added that Turkish press reports that "hit teams were ready for action," were misleading. "Such teams are already deployed by the security forces but their mission is to combat any guerrilla attack within Turkey and not any operation outside the country."[11] Similarly, Turkish President Kenan Evren stated in 1983: "We must be calm. It is they [the Armenian terrorists] who are barbarians. Let the world know that Turkey will have no part in irrational revenge."[12]

It would seem unlikely, therefore, that Turkey is seriously contemplating counterterrorist strikes against Armenian terrorists. Unfounded and inaccurate claims on the part of certain Armenian sources and others concerning "Turkish terrorism," however, obfuscate reality here. The false charges of Turkish conspiracy concerning the attempted assassination and abduction of a number of prominent Armenians are an excellent example of this tendency. Without any proof, Armenian sources have indignantly proclaimed: "Several Armenian centers and monuments have been bombed by Turkish agents in Paris and Beirut. Some young Armenians were assassinated in Holland, Greece, Lebanon and Iran."[13] A similar statement denounced "Turkey's...murder of four alleged ASALA members in parts of Europe."[14]

The French press has generally attributed a number of hostile incidents against Armenians in that country to Turkish groups. In one such case, a so-called "Islamic Turkish Revolutionary Army," claimed credit.[15] Following the bombing of an Armenian memorial in Alfortville, France on May 3, 1984, a man with "an oriental accent" calling from The Hague claimed responsibility on behalf of the "Anti-Armenian Organization."[16] Earlier in 1984, a caller claiming to represent the "Turkish Organization for Armed Struggle" threatened to bomb the French Film Society during the screening of two Armenian movies in Paris. The threat forced the movies to be rescheduled.[17]

Menacing letters signed by a so-called "Third Generation of Black Sea Turks Massacred by Armenian Guerrillas" were received by the Armenian Cultural Center in London.[18] In the summer of 1983, William Lau Richardson, who professed to be a former CIA agent, claimed that a Turkish group in Canada offered him money to kill an Armenian woman in that country as a reprisal for the rash of Armenian terrorist attacks against Turks, but added that he had turned them down.[19] Given Richardson's checkered career, however, it is likely his story was bogus. On October 21, 1984, Levon Ouzounian, one of the wealthiest Armenians living in Cyprus and reputed "to have provided substantial financial assistance to ASALA,"[20] was killed by a hit-and-run driver. The report of the incident "speculated that he [Ouzounian] could have been killed by Turks for his support of ASALA."

More substantial, but still unverified, reports claimed that Dursun Aksoy, the Turkish diplomat assassinated in Brussels, Belgium in July 1983, was "a member of [a] special unit created by Turkish security agencies to track down and kill Armenians suspected of fighting for the underground organization [ASALA]."[21] In addition, ASALA claimed that one of its members, Noubar Yelemian, had been killed in Holland on November 5, 1982, by "Turkish special units assigned to hunting down and killing Armenian terrorists or ASALA members."[22]

The two ASALA members killed by Monte Melkonian's ASALA-RM faction in July 1983 (see above) were initially reported by ASALA as having been "killed by Turks as the result of a tip off by two ASALA informers."[23] Another ASALA report blamed agents of the United States CIA and the Turkish Intelligence Agency (MIT) for the deed. Both agencies were said successfully to have infiltrated anti-Turkish Kurdish groups to carry the operation out.[24]

After he was apprehended for an attempt to bomb the Kuwaiti Airlines office in Athens that instead resulted in the accidental death of his accomplice (Karnik Sarkis Vahradian), Vahe Khudaverdian "insisted that he and his friend were actually targeted by Turkish agents for an assassination."[25] The "ASALA-RM History," written by a dissident ASALA leader however, declared that: "Mujahed [ASALA's leader] fabricated the lie that Karnik and Vahe were the targets of an MIT plot so as to cover-up the real nature of the event." In this case, ASALA-RM's interpretation of ASALA's accusation concerning Turkish counterterror was similar to that of the Greek court because Khudaverdian was found guilty and sentenced to fourteen years in prison.

After thus revealing how ASALA at times deliberately "fabricated...lie[s]" about Turkish counterterror, however, the "ASALA-RM History" did claim that Minas Simonian and Garabed Pashabezian "were most probably the victims of true MIT sponsored plots." Simonian apparently was killed with a silenced pistol in late December of 1982 as he was driving in Beirut, and Pashabezian was killed in March 1983 in his Beirut home. According to the "ASALA-RM History," the identity of both had been revealed by Levon Ekmekjian, the perpetrator of the Ankara airport attack, "as those who helped introduce him to ASALA during his ruthless interrogation and torture by Turkish police before he was hung." In addition, Pashabezian's photo had frequently appeared in ASALA's Beirut organ, *Armenia,* and he also had made public statements on behalf of ASALA.

The Armenian tendency to exaggerate their innocence and the Turks' guilt recently was illustrated by the disappearance of Apo Ashjian, a Dashnak leader in Beirut, Lebanon, on December 29, 1982. On the first anniversary of this occurrence a Dashnak publication carried a front-page article about the matter and included a copy of a telegram sent to President Reagan which charged that Ashjian "was abducted under mysterious circumstances which lead us to believe this unconscionable act was perpetrated by Turkish agents."[26] Another Armenian publication in the United States quickly picked up this issue, also blaming Turkish agents for attempts on the lives of Ara Toranian, an Armenian activist in Paris, France, and Melkon Eblighatian, an Armenian member of the Lebanese parliament. It then declared: "The most prominent example of these Turkish attacks against Armenians took place in Beirut, Dec. 29, 1982...when Abraham Ashjian...was abducted...while on his way to work."[27]

Shortly afterwards, however, a more responsible Armenian publication, revealed that Ashjian probably "was a victim of a power struggle between a left- and a right-wing grouping within the Dashnak party in Lebanon," and added that: "Later the [Dashnak] party made the most of the incident to exploit it for itself and successfully portrayed him [Ashjian] as a victim of Turkish counter terror." The report also indicated that Eblighatian, the Lebanese-Armenian parliamentarian, probably had been involved in similar intramural Dashnak violence.[28]

What is more, Monte Melkonian, the ASALA-RM leader referred to above, stated in an interview with a French journalist that the attempts to kill the French-Armenian leader, Ara Toranian, had been made by ASALA itself. "Hagopian [Mujahed] has liquidated several of our comrades who opposed him. For example, the car of Ara Toranian...was rigged with a bomb by Hagopian's people."[29]

ASALA, however, countered that it was Toranian himself who had bombed the Armenian memorial in Alfortville (see above) in May 1984, not the Turks as was generally believed.[30] Similarly, an explosion, which resulted in minor injuries at the Marie-Nubar Armenian Student Center in Paris on June 23, 1984, was supposedly claimed by "a Turkish underground group."[31] The report of this bombing, however, also revealed that the bombing might also have been the work of "radical [Armenian] students who have openly supported Armenian terrorism" and had had past disputes with the management of the student center. The claim that the Turks were guilty is thus questionable.

On November 29, 1984, a powerful bomb exploded in front of the Salle Pleyel in Paris, an hour before more than 2,000 Armenians were expected to attend a celebration honoring the anniversary of Soviet Armenia.[32] Six Armenians were wounded, two seriously. The Turks, of course, were blamed for the deed. An elderly Armenian, who was in a nearby coffee house, for example, claimed he saw "two suspicious individuals...[who] looked like two young Turkish men" drop "a package and immediately take off." The French police quoted the elderly Armenian as stating: "I am certain they were Turks. I can tell a Turk when I see one." A young Armenian likewise exclaimed: "They definitely are Turks. They killed in the past and they are still murdering."

Since the perpetrators of this bombing have not been apprehended, however, other theories of who did it are equally as plausible. The anti-Soviet Dashnaks, for example, were one of the few Armenian groups in Paris who were not planning to participate in the event. Given the recent spate of intramural Armenian violence mentioned above, the possibility certainly exists that the Dashnaks or some other Armenian group were responsible for the bombing, not the Turks. It would certainly not be the first time that such a scenario of blaming the Turks for intramural Armenian violence had occurred.

Turkish military forces, with the permission of Iraq, did strike at Kurdish and ASALA units in northern Iraq in June 1983. At that time, ASALA claimed "22 of our revolutionaries, including one leading militant, have been lost."[33]

Although official details have never been released, this author understands, through reliable sources in Turkey, that the problem was this. ASALA, operating with the indulgence of Kurds who for all practical purposes were running their own areas in northern Iraq autonomously (the Baghdad government being too preoccupied with fighting the war against Iran), tried to establish a base for operating into Turkey. When the Turks discovered what was happening, they took the issue up with the Iraqis and received a "no objections" to their suggestion that they move in and clean ASALA out, at the same time helping the Iraqis control their Kurdish dissidents.[34]

With Iraqi permission again, a similar Turkish incursion into northern Iraq occurred in October 1984. Published reports indicated that some "250 Armenian men, all members of ASALA...[were] fighting with these Kurdish forces."[35]

With the exception of these two military incursions, however, no definite proof of Turkish counterterrorist activities abroad against Armenians exists. Although the hand of individual, private Turks, embittered by years of contemporary Armenian terrorism, or the acts of official Turkish agents cannot categorically be ruled out in some of these other cases reported above—without any further proof it must be concluded these incidents are just as likely the result of Armenian agents provocateurs, Armenian intramural violence, or some other unexplained causes which might be seeking to perpetuate and/or provoke Turkish-Armenian animosities for their own reasons.

Harassment?—Armenian accusations from outside of Turkey that the Turkish government today harasses, persecutes, and even terrorizes its few (60,000c.) remaining Armenian citizens, pose a somewhat similar, but analytically distinct problem. As with the question of premeditated genocide during World War I, one is again presented with two so diametrically opposed positions that it is difficult to believe they purport to describe the same situation. In this case, however, the question concerns what is happening now, not what occurred seventy years ago, so presumably the facts can be more readily discerned.

The case against Turkey is broadly based: It is asserted Turkish Armenians suffer from cultural, educational, legal, and religious persecution. Armenians and those sympathetic to their cause fill their publications with examples. A few will suffice to illustrate the point. In a wide-ranging analysis, Professor Dickran Kouymjian of California State University, Fresno claimed that contemporary Turkish policy to eliminate Armenian historic monuments takes a number of different forms, including: (1) usage of churches as "convenient targets for artillery practice during maneuvers by the Turkish army in the East," (2) employment of "finely cut stones used on the facades of Armenian churches" by Turkish peasants "in the construction of village dwellings," (3) "conversion of Armenian churches into mosques, prisons, granaries, stables, farms, and museums," (4) "destruction by failure to provide maintenance," (5) "demolition for the construction of roads or public works," and (6) "neutralization of a monument's Armenian identity by the effacing of Armenian inscriptions."[36]

A weekly commentator in one American Armenian newspaper declared "that restrictions on Armenian church properties were endless and ultimately aimed to disappropriate the Armenian community."[37] The

Armenian Patriarch in Istanbul, Shnork Kalustyan, was quoted by a well-known American periodical as stating: "There are bureaucratic discriminations.... We cannot build new churches or repair old ones.... But the Turks can build new mosques.... Our church properties are unfairly taxed.... We are second-class citizens."[38] A young American Armenian law student who recently visited Turkey related how Kalustyan grew so tired of requesting permission from the Turkish government to paint the building which houses the Armenian Patriarchate of Istanbul "that, in an act of desperation, he climbed a ladder and tried to paint it himself. He was stopped by Turkish authorities."[39] Another report told how the Patriarch was prevented from visiting "an Armenian children's camp on the island of Kenali [Kinali]...only a few steps from his own summer residence."[40] Yet another account stated that "Armenian churches and institutions are frequent targets for bomb attacks" and claimed that "many other churches have been converted to barns or museums."[41]

Discussing the present-day plight of Turkish Armenians, "a recent returnee from Turkey" declared: "if they are to live in Turkey, they are forced to change their names.... Their language is forbidden as the language of instruction; the headmaster has to be a Turk."[42] Yet another report explained that the reason "Turks are appointed sub-directors of all Armenian schools...is to 'turkify' the Armenian schools as soon as possible."[43] "Armenian students are not allowed to enter Armenian schools on the pretext that the students are not really Armenians,"[44] affirmed an additional account.

A lengthy update on the present situation in Turkey reported that "during the summer of 1980, a group of Turkish students debarked on the island [of Kinali] shouting insults to the Armenians who were sunbathing there. Witnesses reported that the students threatened and harassed the Armenians who, filled with fright, fled the area. No action was taken against the group of students."[45] Continuing, the same report related that "although few Turks like to admit it...popular opinion would like to see reprisals against the Armenian leaders for the killing of...Turkish diplomatic personnel. 'The Armenians should pack up and get out of Turkey,' one well-known Ankara journalist said."[46]

An eminent American Armenian author, who visited Turkey in the 1970's, claimed that two Armenians were hanged in Erzurum in eastern Turkey after Gourgen Yanikian, a seventy-eight year old Californian of Armenian descent, murdered two Turkish consuls in Los Angeles in 1973. He added that perhaps a dozen more were beaten in Istanbul, one so savagely he no longer could see."[47] As the *National Geographic* article cited above summed it up: "It is the old hatred."[48]

In June 1982, it is claimed, Turkey threatened reprisals against Turkish Jews because Armenian scholars were invited to an international conference in Israel on the Holocaust and other genocides. The Turkish pressure, it is claimed, forced the Israeli government to withdraw its official support from the conference and led to nearly one-third of the 400 registered participants not attending.[49] At the end of 1984, another report asserted that "the

Turkish government resorted without success to extensive measures of pressure, including threats and blackmail [against Turkish Jews], attempting to force the cancellation of several recent lectures sponsored by American Jewish organizations on the Armenian Genocide."[50]

The case of the Turkish Armenian priest, Father Manuel Yergatian (also known as Haig Eldemir), declared one Armenian source in the United States, "is typical of the Turkish government's . . . oppression of Armenians in Turkey."[51] Yergatian was born in Istanbul in 1954. When he was only fourteen, he went to Jerusalem for theological studies at its Armenian Patriarchical Seminary. In 1973, he returned to Turkey to serve his required military obligation. Upon its completion, he was ordained a celibate priest in Istanbul in 1976. The following year he joined the St. James Brotherhood (Sourp Hagop) in Jerusalem.

On October 10, 1980, Father Yergatian was arrested while boarding a plane in Istanbul for Jerusalem. With him were four young Turkish Armenian boys he was taking to Jerusalem to study at its Armenian Patriarchical Seminary. The Turkish authorities charged Yergatian with being involved in activities against the integrity and security of the state. At the time of his arrest he was supposedly carrying cassette tapes of Armenian folk music, a map of historic Armenia, and the address of a well-known terrorist. He also was accused of currency violations and naming one of his dogs "Ataturk." More to the point, the Turkish authorities believed Yergatian was taking the four young students to Jerusalem to have them trained as terrorists. (Sonner Nayir, one of the two Turkish Armenian terrorists convicted of the Orly bombing in 1983, had spent eight years at the same Seminary. The other, Ohannes Semerci, also had studied there.)

During his trial, one of the Jerusalem Seminary students testified Yergatian had taught that eastern Turkey belonged to the Armenians who had been mistreated in 1915 and should have their lands returned. The testimony also indicated that Yergatian had helped decorate the Seminary Hall for observation of Martyrs Day on April 24, 1980.

Armenian sources claim that the charges against Yergatian are trumped up. The "subversive materials" in his possession were simply the autobiography of Father Shigaher, who had described the massacres of 1915, while the map of Armenia was one published by the Mekhitarist fathers of Venice in 1888. The excess money he was charged with carrying simply belonged to the children he was escorting.

The real reason for Yergatian's arrest, feel the Armenians, was his participation in the April 24, 1980 commemoration in Jerusalem. Also, add the same sources, the Turkish authorities were displeased he was rescuing Turkish Armenian "descendants of the survivors of the genocide from Turkification and giving them an opportunity to receive [an] Armenian education in Jerusalem." During his trial, Yergatian himself denied any connection with Armenian terrorism, professed his loyalty to Turkey, and claimed that his imprisonment was in retaliation for Armenian terrorist attacks against Turkish diplomats.

During his long pretrial incarceration, charge Armenian sources,

Yergatian was "reportedly tortured by having his fingernails and toenails pulled out." Finally, after a nine-month-long trial, he was sentenced on March 19, 1983 by the Istanbul Martial Law Command Court to fourteen years imprisonment and five years of internal exile. Recent reports state Yergatian's health has deteriorated in prison and a representative of the Armenian Patriarchate of Istanbul has been refused permission to visit him.

During his visit to the United States in the fall of 1984, Shnork Kalustyan, the Armenian Patriarch of Istanbul who usually assumes a pro-Turkish position, stated that: "Father Yergatian unfortunately had a lot of bad luck during his trials. First of all, he was the victim of baseless accusations by one of his students."[52] In addition, "when Armenian 'terrorists' captured the Turkish consulate in Paris [ASALA's 'Van' operation in September 1981] one of their demands was the release of Father Yergatian, which naturally resulted in his case being subjected to further investigation. . .to see if he belongs to 'ASALA.' This made his case worse." Finally, added the Patriarch, "during his trial, the notorious grave incident took place in Yugoslavia during which a Turkish diplomat [Galip Balkar, March 9, 1983] was assassinated." Thus, concluded Kalustyan, "his only proven guilt is that as a Turkish-Armenian, he had participated in an anti-Turkish rally for which he may have been sentenced to a few years in jail. However, the aforementioned and other incidents, unfortunately, directly or indirectly aggravated his situation."

In May 1983, the famous and highly respected private international organization, Amnesty International (AI), adopted Yergatian as a prisoner of conscience. At that time AI pointed out that the facts of Yergatian's detention and trial made it clear that he had not been convicted of any involvement in violence, but was imprisoned because of his Armenian ethnic origin. In addition, it should be added, a recent AI country report stated about human rights in general in Turkey: "Throughout the year Amnesty International continued to receive allegations that prisoners charged with political offenses had been tortured and that in some cases death had resulted."[53]

Such reports might lend credence to the accusations of Hrant Guzelian, a Turkish Armenian who was one of many witnesses for the defense allowed to testify at the trial of the ASALA group convicted in January 1984 of seizing the Turkish consulate in Paris. Guzelian testified he had been arrested in Turkey on charges he had been forcing Turkish boys to become Armenian. (Guzelian himself claimed that he was simply operating a youth center where Armenian boys brought from the interior of Turkey could be cared for and given educational facilities.) In prison, "he was tortured for a period of 22 days before being transferred."[54] Although he was found innocent for lack of evidence, he claimed "he was once again subjected to extensive beatings, five times within a 24-hour period." This was because, before his release from prison, a soldier recognized him from a news story in a Turkish newspaper which identified him as "an Armenian enemy of Turkey." Only because of the inefficient Turkish bureaucracy, which had not notified the passport authorities of his situation, was he able to leave

Turkey, Guzelian claimed.

Turkish response.—Turks, most Turkish Armenians, and their government paint a very different picture.[55] A recent study of more than fifty Turkish Armenians found them to be "content, prosperous and patriotic to Turkey." Repeatedly, Turkish Armenians emphasized, as did Lucika Martayan, a member of a wealthy industrial family, that "it is the outsiders, those living out of our country, who cause the only trouble we know—whether terrorists or those who don't know the situation here."

The position of Arman Manukyan is also of interest. He is the president of a hardware and tool company, a full professor of accounting at the University of the Bosphorus in Istanbul, and a member of the Turkish Foreign Minister's Advisory Committee on Foreign Relations. In 1958, he received a two-year Fulbright Scholarship to study in the United States where his first child was born. His wife, Alis, is a leading soprano in the Istanbul State Opera. Some twenty other Armenians sing in the opera chorus. All were trained for free at Turkish state conservatories.

Manukyan himself visits the United States annually. "I could live anywhere in the world," he declared, but "I want to live here. Why shouldn't I? It is my home country. And I think my son will return to live here, too, after he finishes his American education." Concerning the Muslim Turks, Manukyan stated that "we live as brothers without separation or difference...Christians and Muslims are not so different in our basic morals. We have the same life patterns and the same values here."

Regarding the Armenian terrorists, Manukyan declared that they "could not have come out of our life here, which is peaceful and happy." He added that "we have 33 of our own churches, 30 schools, our own sport and cultural clubs and halls, our own alumni associations. Life is liberal and free here. We don't feel any pressures. If we did, most of us would leave."

Karabet Arman, the chief physician at the Yedikule Armenian Hospital in Istanbul, said the Muslim Turks and Turkish Armenians are *"kardes gibi,"* or "like brothers." He told how he had been trained in the Istanbul University Medical School. "In the 30 years since, I have been the head of three university clinics as well as the medical director of several prominent businesses." He added that "the Armenian doctors are given full scholarships in Turkey and also all expenses to study in Germany, England, and the United States, like the Turks." Although he often visits his brother in the United States, Arman declared that he did not want to emigrate. He also affirmed that Armenian churches are open every day, that Armenians feel equal and safe in the midst of the Muslim majority, and that during the religious festivals, "the bells of our churches ring so loud that even the voices of the *muezzin* [the Muslim cleric who calls the faithful to prayer] will be drowned in it."

Ara Kuyumcuyan heads large iron, steel, and concrete companies. Hundreds of Turks work for him. In an interview, he declared: "My father was born in Istanbul. We Armenians have a very good life in Turkey.... We live in peace." Another wealthy businessman, who said terrorists had threatened and blackmailed Armenians in foreign countries, asked that his name not be used. He stated that "all people are equal here. . . . There is no attempt to discriminate. . . . Life is *cok, cok iyi*—very, very good here." Still another Armenian studying electronic engineering in Switzerland was home for the summer. He too had friends who had been threatened by terrorists in Switzerland, but declared: "I definitely plan to return to Turkey to live and work. . . . I feel that I have a great future in Turkey in computers."

Calouste Gulbenkyan, the late oil magnate, was quoted as saying: "Today in Turkey no distinction whatsoever is made between the Turks and the Armenians. The Turkish Armenians live peacefully and in prosperity." Krikor Gunbeyan, a shoemaker, stated: "There is no discrimination among the citizens of the Republic of Turkey because of difference in language, religion and race."

In reply to the foreign Armenian accusation that Turkish Armenians are afraid to tell the truth, the writer, Torkom Istepanyan, declared: "I may be accused of being a 'hireling' by some persons outside the country. Let them understand clearly that the blood in my veins is at least as much Armenian as theirs. In fact, it is the very purity of my blood that compels me to be faithful to the truth, and the truth is that we Turkish Armenians with our independent churches and community schools, live here in an atmosphere of complete freedom, far removed from futile vendettas."

Ironically, the Armenian Patriarch in Istanbul, who was quoted above as criticizing the situation in Turkey, stated that: "The young people, the terrorists, have been exposed to misrepresentations. They have been fed distorted views on what happened in 1915." He went on to tell how under the Turkish Republic the Armenians, like the other minorities in Turkey, have all the freedoms and responsibilities of citizenship. He even volunteered that the Turkish Armenians recently rebuilt the handsome new cathedral of St. Gregory the Illuminator in the heart of Istanbul's business district.

During his visit to the United States in 1984, the Armenian Patriarch similarly stated: "Our government insures our freedom and safety and gone are some of the restrictions that had existed in the past relative to the day-to-day life of our community organizations."[56] When Armenian terrorists kill Turkish diplomats abroad, added Kaloustyan, "the Turkish government immediately takes measures to provide protection for us by posting policemen at Armenian institutions to prevent any retaliation."

During the trial for the Orly bombers in March 1985, Professor Simon A. Hatchinlian, a Turkish Armenian lecturer at the University of the Bosphorus, testified for the prosecution. He "noted that as an Armenian living in Turkey, he has never been discriminated against from the time he served in the Turkish Army to the present."[57] Hatchinlian added "that he uses an Armenian name without anyone telling him to change it, enjoys all types of privileges granted to all Turkish citizens and that he has the respect of all his Turkish colleagues."

Synthesis.—What then is the actual position of the Armenians in Turkey today? It is true that Republican Turkish policies towards minorities have not always achieved the laic ideal. (What country has?) The claim in the 1920's that the Kurds were simply "mountain Turks," the notorious *Varlik Vergisi* (Capital Levy) of 1942-43 which blatantly discriminated against minorities, the anti-Greek riots over Cyprus in September 1955, and the Kurdish unrest in eastern Turkey during the 1980's are illustrative. What is more, of course, Republican Turkey only arose from the ashes of the Ottoman Empire after a desperate war against the Greeks in the West, and a lesser but still serious war against the Armenians in the East. Indeed, their deaths from this latter conflict are counted by the Armenians today when they number their loses during what they claim was the Turkish genocide against them.

Turkish sensitivities about minorities and a desire to have a Turkey for the Turks is understandable, however, given the former Empire's loss of vast amounts of territory in the past, the resulting forced migrations of Muslims from these lands to Anatolia, and the attempts by the Greeks and the Armenians—as well as the Allies—after World War I to carve out large sections of Anatolia for themselves. Turks came late to the idea of a nation-state, but after it had helped to destroy their multinational empire and threatened the very existence of their Anatolian heartland, they too learned to value one for themselves.

Certainly, it would not be reasonable to expect the residue of attitudes in Turkish society, which in the past resulted in de facto discrimination and sometimes hostile behavior, to be eradicated overnight any more than it proved possible to eliminate racial prejudices in the United States after the Civil War. In the Turkish case, as in the United States, however, practice has come to conform with law over time. There have been no outbreaks of anti-minority violence on any significant scale in Turkey for thirty years despite the actions of Armenian terrorists who have tried to foment it. Given the history of Armenian-Turkish relations in the past, especially as viewed from the Turkish perspective, the position of the Armenians in Turkey today is probably much better than could otherwise be expected.

Unofficial pressures to conform culturally and religiously undoubtedly exist in Turkey today, but how is this different than in any other country? The situation in Turkey is certainly not unique. In actual practice, despite the protestations of Armenians abroad, those in Turkey are probably better off than their co-ethnics in such other middle eastern countries as Iran and Syria.

As for the numerous bureaucratic problems Armenians face in Turkey today, these are often difficulties from which Muslim Turks too suffer. As anyone—native or foreign—who has dealt with it can attest, the Turkish bureaucracy is far from being the most efficient. This is regrettable, but in most cases probably not a valid criticism as far as the Armenian minority goes. Indeed, in the case of Hrant Guzelian, the Turkish Armenian who testified at the 1984 trial in Paris of the four ASALA agents, the inefficiencies of the Turkish bureaucracy apparently came to his aid. In short, therefore, these bureaucratic problems (which may often appear to be harassment to outsiders) are endemic to the country, not peculiarly aimed at just one minority grouping. The solution lies in education and reform, not in biased diatribes.

What about the charges that ancient Armenian churches and other historical monuments are being allowed to fall into ruin or being otherwise mistreated? Although it is true that contemporary Turkish studies downplay the historical Armenian presence in eastern Anatolia, there can be absolutely no doubt that the governments of Republican Turkey have made strenuous efforts to preserve their vast archeological heritage. Anyone who has visited the country can attest to this fact. While isolated incidents of vandalism may occur and adequate funds for preservation are not always available, there is no evidence that the Turkish government is destroying historical Armenian churches and monuments as an official policy. On the contrary, as even foreign Armenians who visit Turkey can testify—historical Armenian sites in eastern Anatolia and ancient Cilicia are being preserved and protected better than might be expected for a country which is not yet blessed with all the necessary required means the more fortunate might possess.

At Aghtamar, for example, the famous island in Lake Van which once was the center of an independent Armenian Catholicosate, efforts recently have been made at maintenance and landscaping.[58] Numerous tourists come to see the magnificent Armenian Church built more than 1000 years ago. The Turkish military has even built a helicopter pad on the island to facilitate VIP visits. The ancient Armenian capital of Ani, right on the Soviet border, is readily accessible, and the military, who control the area, provide permits and escorts for visitors. A number of French Armenians, among others, visit the site annually. The Armenian Cathedral in Kars has recently been cleaned up and restored.

On the other hand, some Armenian churches are still used for storing hay or firewood, and as stables. The complex on Mt. Varag east of Van is a case in point. But this is no different from the condition of numerous former Christian churches of denominations other than Armenian in many parts of Anatolia. In addition, one does not have to search far to find abandoned mosques, caravanserais, and great complexes of Muslim tombs, such as the ones at Ahlat on the northwestern shore of Lake Van, which are also in a sad state of neglect. Turkey has so many historical monuments that the entire national budget could be spent in any given year on their restoration and maintenance. Given the poor state of overall Turkish-Armenian relations during the past century and the economic problems of Turkey in recent years, the wonder is that so many historical monuments, including Armenian ones, are so well preserved and maintained. Armenian allegations to the contrary are specious, but they feed on themselves. Armenians living abroad believe them because they are fed a steady diet of disinformation, distortion, and outright falsehoods.

How about the accusation that the Turkish government threatened reprisals against Turkish Jews if Jewish organizations in the United States or an Israeli conference in Tel Aviv permitted Armenians to present lectures and papers on the Armenian genocide? According to an apparently reliable

Turkish source,[59] the charges concerning such events in the United States are baseless. All the Turks attempted to do here was to request that Jewish organizations not permit Armenians to participate in conferences about the Jewish Holocaust or genocide in general. No threats, either overt or implied, were made. Regarding the 1982 conference in Israel, however, a certain Turkish official did make unauthorized pronouncements which might have been construed as threats. When this was discovered, the Turkish government disowned the statements.

Finally, how might the situation of Father Yergatian and others, whom Amnesty International has commented upon, be explained? First of all, of course, Turkey is not a completely Westernized country. Despite the westernization that has occurred since the inception of the Republic, cultural norms concerning what is and is not proper treatment of prisoners inevitably differ from the West. Torture does occur (although not to the extent some claim). This may be regrettable for Westerners raised with different values, but ought to be understandable,[60] especially since, in most cases, it does not appear to be official governmental policy. Indeed, the government disciplines those who are discovered to be using it.[61]

Furthermore, since Turkey is a democracy, it is more open than most other countries. Reports about prison conditions can be more readily made. To the superficial observer, therefore, it may seem that the situation may be worse than in many closed societies when in reality, of course, the flow of information is simply much less in these latter places.

In closing, one must realize that in the late 1970's, Turkey was in the grips of a vicious cycle of leftist-rightist terrorism that was claiming almost thirty lives per day, had brought some sectors of the economy to a standstill, and had seen the entire country overcome by fear. At last, on September 12, 1980, the military stepped in to restore order and began to pull the country back from the brink of collapse.[62]

It was not easy. To paraphrase Abraham Lincoln, it might have been necessary to amputate a limb in order to save the body. Nobody pretends that the military used kid gloves. Few wanted it to. The public support for General Kenan Evren's measures was phenomenal. Even more incredible, moreover, was the relative leniency the military government showed towards those accused of terrorism. It is extremely doubtful a house in such terroristic disorder could have been set in order so lightly as was done after 1980.

Even more noteworthy, however, was the Turkish military's attitude towards genuine democracy. Despite dire predictions and much hypocritical criticism from the West, the military government held elections in November 1983 that resulted in the party it favored, placing last, while the one it preferred least, Turgut Ozal's Motherland Party, winning an impressive victory. True to the dictates of Ataturk, the military, having reinstituted a stable democracy, stepped aside and permitted Ozal to assume power. Given the inherent difficulties involved, it would be very difficult to find a more impressive track record concerning democracy and the values Westerners associate with it. In conclusion, therefore, while isolated examples of prejudices and persecution against Armenians undoubtedly exist among the Muslim majority—the case against Father Yergatian might be one such example—there can be no doubt that today the Turkish Armenians enjoy a wide degree of real equality and prosperity.

Notes

[1]There are two main Armenian terrorist groups. The Armenian Secret Army for the Liberation of Armenia (ASALA) is a Marxist organization. In 1983, some of its members violently broke away to form ASALA-Revolutionary Movement (ASALA-RM). The other group, the Justice Commandos of the Armenian Genocide (JCAG), was created by the nationalist Armenian Revolutionary Federation (ARF) or Dashnaks, a political party first established in 1890. Due to intra-Dashnak violence, the ARF renamed its terrorist arm the Armenian Revolutionary Army (ARA) in 1983. For an in-depth analysis of Armenian terrorism, see Michael M. Gunter, *"Pursuing the Just Cause of their People": A Study of Contemporary Armenian Terrorism* (Westport, Connecticut: Greenwood Press, 1986).

[2]Cited in *Christian Science Monitor*, May 7, 1982, p. 5.

[3]Cited in *Turkish Daily News*, August 30, 1982, p. 3.

[4]Cited in *Los Angeles Times*, July 16, 1983, p. 17.

[5]"Report on Armenian Conference in Lausanne: London *Al-Dustur* in Arabic, August 8, 1983, p. 35," in *Joint Publications Research Service: Armenian Affairs*, No. 2831, October 3, 1983, p. 16.

[6]Thomas C. Goltz, "Armenian Terror Rouses Turkish Liberal Anger," *The Daily Star* [Beirut, Lebanon], December 5, 1984, as cited in *The Armenian Weekly*, January 12, 1985, p. 2.

[7]Robert Kaplan, "Armenian Terrorists Find New Bases from which to Wage Their Battle for a Homeland," *Christian Science Monitor*, July 14, 1983, p. 12.

[8]Cited in *New York Times*, February 28, 1980, p. A3.

[9]Cited in Kaplan, "Armenian Terrorists Find New Bases."

[10]*Ibid.*

[11]Cited in *Turkish Daily News*, August 30, 1982, p. 1.

[12]Cited in Goltz, "Armenian Terror Rouses Turkish Anger."

[13]*The [Armenian] California Courier*, November 16, 1983, p. 4.

[14]Aram H. Kailian, "Is Anyone Listening?" *The Armenian Weekly*, September 3, 1983, p. 2.

[15]See *The Armenian Reporter*, May 10, 1984, p. 14.

[16]*The Armenian Weekly*, May 12, 1984, p. 1.

[17]"Turkish Terror," *The [Armenian] California Courier*, February 16, 1984, p. 2.

[18]"Turkish Threats," in *Ibid.*, March 1, 1984, p. 2.

[19]See the reports in *The Armenian Reporter*, August 11, 1983, p. 11; and *The [Armenian] California Courier*, August 25, 1983, p. 8.

[20]For this and the following citation, see "ASALA Supporter Said to have been Killed by Hit & Run Car on Cyprus," *The Armenian Reporter*, December 6, 1984, p. 12.

[21]*The Armenian Reporter*, September 8, 1983, p. 13. Also see *Ibid.*, January 5, 1984, p. 1.

[22]*Ibid.*, August 11, 1983, p. 14.

[23]*Ibid.*, September 8, 1983, p. 16.

[24]*Ibid.*, September 22, 1983, p. 8.

[25]See "ASALA Man Given 14 Years for Attack on Kuwait Airways in Athens," in *Ibid.*, January 31, 1985, p. 1.

[26]*The Armenian Weekly*, January 7, 1984, p. 1.

[27]Harut Sassounian, "Turkish Anti-Hye Threats Should Not Be Ignored," *The [Armenian] California Courier*, January 19, 1984, p. 4.

[28]"New Light Shed on Kidnapping of ARF Leader in December of 1982," *The Armenian Reporter*, January 26, 1984, pp. 1, 8. Also see *The Armenian Reporter*, June 7, 1984, p. 1. For additional examples of intramural Armenian violence over the years, see Robert Mirak, *Torn Between Two Lands: Armenians in America, 1890 to World War I* (Cambridge: Harvard University Press, 1983), pp. 231-2, 240, & 245-7; and K.S. Papazian, *Patriotism Perverted* (Boston: Baikar Press, 1934), pp. 15-6, 60-5, & 68-73.

[29]Cited in *The Armenian Reporter*, January 12, 1984, p. 4.

[30]For this claim see "ASALA Discloses Names of Former Members Involved in Various Acts," in *Ibid.*, September 13, 1984, p. 12.

[31]For the details of this event, see "Armenian Students' Center in Paris is Target of Bombing by Turkish Group," *Ibid.*, August 9, 1984, p. 13.

[32]This and the following details are mostly taken from the report in *The Armenian Reporter*, November 29, 1984, p. 1.

[33]"Secret Army Indicates a Loss of 22 Members in Border Skirmish," in *Ibid.*, June 16, 1983, p. 1. Also see Sam Cohen, "Turkey's Mysterious Strike in Iraq Underlines Ongoing Effort to Uproot Kurdish Nationalism," *Christian Science Monitor*, July 14, 1983, p. 12.

[34]The following explanation, which dovetails with media reports at the time, comes from reliable Turkish sources which prefer not to be cited directly.

[35]See the reports on this Turkish military strike in *The Armenian Reporter,* October 25, 1984, p. 1; and *The Armenian Weekly,* November 3, 1984, p. 1, 12.

[36]*The [Armenian] California Courier,* May 31, 1984, p. 1.

[37]Harut Sassounian, "Turkish-Armenians Live Deprived of Their Rights," in *Ibid.,* December 8, 1983, p. 4.

[38]Robert Paul Jordan, "The Proud Armenians," *National Geographic* 153 (June 1978), p. 851. See also the Patriarch's statement concerning "Restrictions on the Armenian Community in Turkey (1974)" in David Marshall Lang and Christopher J. Walker, *The Armenians* (London: Minority Rights Group Ltd., 1981), pp. 21-22.

[39]*The Armenian Weekly,* November 5, 1983, p. 2.

[40]*The Armenian Reporter,* January 19, 1984, p. 2.

[41]*The [Armenian] California Courier,* December 8, 1983, pp. 4-5.

[42]Cited in *The Armenian Weekly,* July 16, 1983, p. 10.

[43]Cited in *Ibid.,* December 17, 1983, p. 11.

[44]*The [Armenian] California Courier,* December 8, 1983, p. 4.

[45]Cited in *The Armenian Weekly,* December 31, 1983, p. 7.

[46]*Ibid.*

[47]Michael Arlen, *Passage to Ararat* (New York: Farrar, Straus & Giroux, 1975), p. 285.

[48]Jordan, "The Proud Armenians," p. 847.

[49]See the accounts in the *New York Times,* June 3, 1982, p. 1; and *The Armenian Reporter,* October 11, 1984, p. 12. See also, however, the Turkish reply in the *New York Times,* June 5, 1982, p. 3.

[50]See "Turkey Pressures Jews to Silence Armenians," *The [Armenian] California Courier,* January 31, 1985, pp. 1, 11.

[51]*The Armenian Reporter,* November 3, 1983, p. 15. Unless otherwise stated, the following discussion is based on the lengthy report in *The [Armenian] California Courier,* January 26, 1984, pp. 1, 11; *Ibid.,* April 26, 1984, p. 4; *The Armenian Reporter,* November 24, 1983, p. 10; *Ibid.,* November 17, 1983, p. 14; and *Ibid.,* October 4, 1984, pp. 16-17.

[52]The following citations are taken from "Patriarch of Turkey Calls Father Yergatian a Victim," *The [Armenian] California Courier,* November 7, 1984, pp. 1, 10.

[53]*Amnesty International Report* 1983 (London: Amnesty International Publications, 1983), pp. 281-2. Also see *Torture in the Eighties* (London: Amnesty International Publications, 1984), pp. 217-220; and various other AI bulletins and reports concerning human rights violations in Turkey today. In addition see by Helsinki Watch, "Human Rights in Turkey's 'Transition to Democracy,' " (November 3, 1983); and "Straws in the Wind: Prospects for Human Rights and Democracy in Turkey," (July 1984); as well as the following MERIP Reports: "Turkey: The Generals Take Over," (No. 93, January 1981); "State Terror in Turkey," (No. 121, February 1984); and "Turkey Under Military Rule," (No. 122, March/April 1984).
Since the materials cited here concern the general situation in Turkey and not the specific condition of the Armenians, they are beyond the scope of my present inquiry. In addition, of course, they do not reflect the official Turkish position or explanations. Nevertheless, I have cited them in the interest of being as thorough as possible.

[54]This citation and the following information were taken from *The Armenian Reporter,* February 16, 1984, p. 14.

[55]Unless otherwise noted, the following discussion is largely based on "Armenians Attest to Happy and Prosperous Life in Turkey, Speak Out Against Terrorism," *Los Angeles Times,* November 12, 1982, Part 1-B, pp. 8, 9; and also on Ralph J. Kaplan, "In Turkey, Armenians Put the Past Behind Them," *Los Angeles Herald Examiner,* November 23, 1983, p. A11; and *Facts From the Turkish Armenians* (Istanbul: Jamanak, 1980).

[56]This and the following citation are taken from *The Armenian Reporter,* November 15, 1984, p. 1.

[57]This and the following citation are taken from "Istanbul Armenian Testifies for the Prosecution in Paris," in *Ibid.,* March 14, 1985, p. 17.

[58]I would like to thank Paul B. Henze, who has travelled widely and frequently throughout Turkey for a number of years and is presently a foreign affairs consultant for the Rand Corporation, for much of the information upon which my following discussion is based.

[59]The source of this information appears reliable, but prefers to remain anonymous.

[60]In general, see Adda B. Bozeman, *The Future of Law in a Multicultural World* (Princeton: Princeton University Press, 1971).

[61]For the official position of the Turkish government, see *The Human Rights Situation in Turkey: Facts vs. Allegations* (Ankara: Prime Ministry Directorate General of Press and Information, [1984]).

[62]For pithy analyses, see Lucille W. Pevsner, *Turkey's Political Crisis: Background, Perspectives, Prospects* (New York: Praeger, 1984); and C.H. Dodd, *The Crisis of Turkish Democracy* (North Humberside, England: The Eothen Press, 1983).

Iran: Revolution, Culture, and Collective Action

8

GREGORY F. ROSE

It is possible to argue, as Theda Skocpol did in her retrospective analysis of the Iranian revolution, that the Islamic revolution in Iran represents a fundamentally new type of revolution, a type which, precisely because of its novel introduction of "the possible role of idea systems and cultural understandings in the shaping of political action,"[1] escapes hitherto-developed analytical categories. Such a view, however, is misleading. It is misleading precisely because the novelty in the Iranian case is not *typological*.

The novelty in the Iranian case is the degree to which this revolution highlights the relationship between culture and collective action. The Iranian case merely exhibits in a more striking and unmistakeable fashion a dynamic which is common to all revolutions, but which structural analysis of the causes of revolution obscures because of assumptions such analysts tend to make concerning a particular kind of collective action — revolutionary mobilization. Specifically, structural analysis of the causes of revolutions assumes that economic outcomes associated with structural causes are the necessary and, usually, sufficient conditions for revolutionary mobilization. In the Iranian case strictly economic incentives, while present, were clearly of tertiary importance.[2] The fact that economic outcomes were not generally the source of revolutionary mobilization in Iran does not suggest that Iran's revolution is a new type; rather it suggests that the problem of revolutionary mobilization is a serious collective action problem and that the economic-determinist assumptions carried in structural analyses simply ignore the collective action problem by postulation of *strictly* economic incentives for revolutionary mobilization.

What the case of Iran does provide is additional insight into the ways in which collective action problems can be addressed. It raises the question of whether culture — broadly defined — can condition an environment in which the problem of revolutionary mobilization as collective action can be rendered less intractable. The problem, to be sure, with culture as a variable is that culture, by definition varies little over long periods of time. In the case of Iran, however, one can see the impact of the cultural variable by observing the relationship between changes of residency patterns of certain "culture-bearers" and their amenability to revolutionary mobilization.

The general framework used for this analysis is that developed by Samuel Popkin in his study of the Vietnamese revolution.[3] Popkin argues that shifting the focus of analysis from aggregates to individuals permits greater insight into the ways in which revolutionary movements mobilize a mass base for seizing state power. Key to this shift of analysis is consideration of the problem posed by Mancur Olson in his general study of collective action, the problem of the free rider. Two assumptions characterize actors where the free rider problem emerges — rationality (the actor discerns

73

open alternatives and is capable of rank-ordering alternative courses of action in terms of maximizing some preferred utility) and egoism (the actor most prefers that utility which most realizes his self-interest).[4] Two assumptions also characterize collective goods susceptible to the free rider problem — the impossibility of excluding noncontributors and the jointness of the goods' supply. In brief, the rational actor will choose that course of action which imposes no costs upon himself if the collective action of others produces a good from which he cannot be excluded, regardless of his noncontribution — the problem which Olson identifies becomes the fact that:

> ...unless there is coercion or some other special device to make individuals act in their common interest, rational, self-interested individuals will not act to achieve their common or group interest.[5]

Olson suggests that the use of such special devices which produce excludable goods for individuals can induce willingness on the part of rational-egoist actors to engage in collective action. This view is termed the "by-product" theory of collective goods. Popkin expands on Olson's original analysis by suggesting that:

> Contributions can occur (1) because persons contribute for reasons of ethics, conscience, or altruism; (2) because it pays to contribute on a pure cost-benefit basis; (3) because of selective incentives (excludable benefits), which can be either positive or negative; or (4) because it pays to contribute, given that the contributions of others are contingent on one's own contribution.[6]

In analyzing the Vietnamese revolution, Popkin suggests that peasants, as rational-egoist actors, evaluate risks of participation in revolutionary movements in terms of the ability of these movements to provide selective incentives, the degree to which the leadership of such movements is credible, and the degree to which individual participation is a condition of contribution by others.

The role of the political entrepreneur, as Popkin terms the revolutionary leadership, is pivotal. The mobilizing success of the political entrepreneur is conditioned by the degree to which he communicates in terms and symbols which his target audience understands, he presents a credible vision of the future, he embodies a persuasive moral code (frequently involving self-abnegation), he is familiar as a figure of authority to the target audience, and he can provide "local goods and goods with immediate payoffs" to convince the target audience of his efficacy.[7]

In applying Popkin's framework to the Iranian case, I shall concentrate on revolutionary events in Tehran in the period August 1978 to February 1979.[8] The vast majority of Tehran's urban poor, concentrated primarily in the southern half of the city, consisted of either first- or second-generation peasant migrants to the city who frequently maintained close social and economic links to the peasant communities from which they emigrated.[9] Thus, if Popkin's analysis of the constraints on peasant behavior imposed by village life is correct, one might expect Iran's recently-urbanized peasants to exhibit approximations of the behavior Popkin predicts. While the anthropological literature on recently-urbanized peasants in Iran is sparse, what literature exists suggests striking parallels to Popkin's model of peasant behavior; even more striking is the parallel between anthropological studies of peasant behavior in villages in Iran and Popkin's observations in Vietnam. Furthermore, survey-research studies of peasant motivations for emigration to urban centers in Iran strongly suggests that threat to subsistence was less a motivation than anticipation of a higher standard of living available even to unskilled day-laborers in urban centers.[10] Thus, recently-urbanized peasants in Iran exhibited no great risk-aversion, but precisely the rational risk calculation which Popkin predicts.

The question which acutely arises is: why did these recently-urbanized peasants become mobilized as the vast majority of active participants in the revolutionary movement? What special incentives might have induced this collective action and, more specifically, what special incentives might have induced collective action of the particular type which occurred in Tehran? This second question is significant in light of the gross disparity in recently-urbanized peasant participation in revolutionary demonstrations organized by the left and the National Front and those organized by the religious opposition; a call from the left or the National Front might produce a demonstration of fifty thousand to two-hundred and fifty thousand persons; a call from Imam Khomeini put two to four million into the streets.

I suggest that recently-urbanized peasants chose to accept the leadership of Imam Khomeini and the religious opposition because that revolutionary leadership possessed more credible political entrepreneurs and provided a strong special incentive, the by-product of which was collective revolutionary action.

Analyzing the religious opposition's leadership, and that of Imam Khomeini in particular, a compelling case can be made for this proposition. Anthropological and political observers have frequently commented on Khomeini's use of terms, symbols and a speaking style which communicated more effectively with the peasant audience than any other figure in the opposition (Khomeini's radio-broadcast speeches are delivered with a strong rural accent and grammatical constructions which are more common to the language of the lower social classes, and the peasant in particular, than upper-class "literary" Persian). A content analysis of the speeches of Khomeini and other religious opposition leaders in the pre-revolutionary period indicates a high correlation between the semantic fields employed by these leaders and their recently-urbanized peasant audience. The vision of the future presented by Imam Khomeini, portrayed as it was in traditional and religious imagery, was more credible than any non-religious, particularly Western, vision, the substance of which was, at best, incomprehensible to the recently-urbanized peasant and, at worst, deeply offensive. Similarly, Imam Khomeini in particular embodied a demanding moral code, the substance of which was shared by the recently-urbanized peasant audience, and Imam Khomeini's ascetic image stood in stark contrast to much of the imperial elite and competing revolutionary leaderships (this contention can be called into question with respect to other figures in the leadership of the religious opposition — however, Imam Khomeini, by and large, symbolized the religious leadership for the target audience). Furthermore, the religious leadership was, indeed, familiar to the recently-urbanized peasant as a source of authority (the seniormost religious leaders, including Imam Khomeini, were known as the *maraji'-i taqlid* — "sources of emulation" — and every believer, to the extent that he is not himself an expert in Islamic jurisprudence, is obligated in Shi'i Islam to emulate such a source in matters of religious practice, an institution known as *marja'iyyat*).

The fifth characteristic of effective political entrepreneurship — provision of local goods and goods with immediate payoffs — is less evident in the Iranian case (and this is to an extent a consequence of the fact that the Vietnamese case from which Popkin derived his model involved prolonged guerrilla warfare, while the Iranian case was of far shorter duration and was a largely urban affair). However, it can be plausibly argued that the provision of social welfare, through *sadaqat* (charity) and *khoms* (a kind of unofficial religious tax administered by the *maraji'-i taqlid*) distributed by the local mosques, after the collapse of the unskilled construction labor market in Tehran in 1975-76 constituted such a local good with an immediate payoff, particularly in light of the absence of a state-organized welfare system. Still, this local good was certainly far less in scope and impact than the local goods provided by Vietnamese revolutionaries.

The special incentive provided by the religious opposition was, simply put, salvation. As Popkin himself notes, "...the quintessential excludables often involve religion."[12] In the case of Shi'i Islam, the strong identification of salvific faith with action to embody that faith, suggested by the jurisprudential definition of *iman* (faith) as *tasdiq* (realization of God's will on earth), conditioned salvation on behavior which aimed at realizing God's intended polity on earth.[13] This was reinforced, no doubt, by the traditional institution of *marja'iyyat*. Once the attention of the recently-urbanized peasant was drawn by the religious leadership to the claimed entailment of revolutionary action by the basic tenets of the faith, revolutionary mobilization rapidly occurred.

To be sure, Imam Khomeini had made such a call in 1963 and, while the imperial regime was sorely tested by the ensuing clashes, no successful revolutionary mobilization took place. I suggest that the difference in 1978-79 was in the concentration of the target audience in urban centers which took place in the period 1964-1978 and which permitted considerably more effective communication between the leadership of the religious opposition and the target audience. Table 1 shows the distribution of population in Iran's ten largest cities in 1966 and 1976. Tehran's population alone increased by nearly 40% in that ten year period.[14] Table 2 indicates that rural-to-urban migration throughout Iran accounted for 35.2% of the urban population increase in the same period, with an average annual increase of 211,000 during the period attributed to rural-to-urban migration. A peasant population, thus, was concentrated from the relative diffused environment of Iran's 60,000 villages to a few urban centers, of which the most prominent was Tehran. In these centers, these urbanized peasants increasingly turned to their cultural tradition, in particular Shi'i Islam, in response to the anomie they experienced in the urban environment.[15] This concentration in urban centers of a population culturally-conditioned to religious appeals, coupled with the increasing stature of Imam Khomeini as a religious leader (Popkin's fourth criterion of political entrepreneurship) as he became almost exclusively identified as the source of religious opposition to the imperial regime, provided the key difference between 1963 and 1978-79.

Application of Popkin's framework to the Iranian case highlights, then, the interesting way in which the Iranian revolution resolved the collective action problem presented to it and sets the basis for a rather more interesting theoretical point.

TABLE 1
Population Distribution in Iran's Ten Largest Cities

City	1966	1976
Tehran	2,719,730	4,496,159
Isfahan	424,045	671,825
Mashhad	409,616	670,180
Tabriz	403,413	598,576
Shiraz	269,865	416,408
Ahvaz	206,375	329,006
Abadan	272,962	296,081
Kermanshah	187,930	290,861
Qom	134,292	246,831
Rasht	143,557	187,203

Source: Adapted from Kazemi, *Poverty and Revolution in Iran*, p. 17.

TABLE 2
Increase in Iranian Urban Population: 1966-1976

	Total Population (000)	Percent of Total Increase	Average Annual Increase (000)
Natural Population Increase	2,621	43.7	262
Rural to Urban Migration	2,111	35.2	211

Source: Adapted from Kazemi, *Poverty and Revolution in Iran*, p 14.

Similar to the "free rider" problem of collective action is the problem of the "Prisoners' Dilemma." Here it is shown that under certain conditions rational-egoist actors will be unable to reach a Pareto-optimal solution to their dilemma, despite the convergence of their interests. The following matrix illustrates the problem (where R is the reward, P is the punishment, T is the utility accruing to defection, and S is the "sucker" payoff):

		Prisoner A's Choice:	
		COOPERATE	DEFECT
B's Choice		COOPERATE	R,R (3,3)	S,T (1,4)
		DEFECT	T,S (4,1)	P,P (2.2)
Payoff Ordering:		T > R > P > S	Condition: R > (S + T)/2	

In this game, both prisoners would be worse off by defecting than by cooperating, but each ranks the utility accruing to defection higher in his own self-interest than the utility of cooperation. When one adds, however, certain additional assumptions, this outcome is no longer so clear. For example, if one assumes that both prisoners are members of *Cosa Nostra,* sworn to the oath of silence — *omerta* — and aware that defection would likely result in the defector's murder at the hands of other organization members, the subjective game matrix for the prisoners would be:

		Prisoner A:	
		COOPERATE	DEFECT
Prisoner B:		COOPERATE	R,R (4,4)	S,T (3,2)
		DEFECT	T,S (2,3)	P,P (1,1)

Thus, introduction of an assumption about prior relations of power, expectation, values and conventions can radically change the expected outcome by predisposing the players to cooperation. Such outcomes have been generally noted with respect to repeated-iteration games. As Alexander Field suggests, rational-choice analysis has precisely to make assumptions about such factors which affect how interests are determined and, consequently, how calculations about interests are made.[16]

This excursus into the "Prisoners' Dilemma" highlights the general theoretical contribution of the Iranian case. If the problem of revolutionary mobilization is a free rider problem, then the intractability of such a free rider problem is conditioned by the ways in which prior factors affect determination of interests by actors and the ways in which actors make calculations about their interests. This complex of prior factors is the "web of significance" which Clifford Geertz has defined as "culture:" "a context, something within which [social events] can be intelligibly described."[17] At least four of Popkin's criteria of effective political entrepreneurship (communicative skill, shared vision, persuasive moral codes, and familiarity of authority) point to the effect of culture on overcoming the problem of collective action. Furthermore, it is reasonable to suppose that cultures wherein which special incentives are plentiful or a certain special incentive is especially prized or a particular culture-bearing population is especially available to political entrepreneurs provide environments wherein the problem of collective action can be more easily surmounted. This certainly seems to be the case for Iran.

This analysis brings us full circle to the observation that structural analyses of the causes of revolution fail to explain the Iranian case because of their economic-determinist assumptions about collective action. The Iranian case, certainly, does not suggest that extra-economic phenomena lie at the root of all revolutionary mobilization; rather, it underscores the importance of the problem of collective action and, while economic special incentives may be present in some cases, the cultural environment can, and in the case of Iran does, provide equally compelling special incentives. The question becomes, then, an empirical one.

Notes

[1]Theda Skopol, "The Rentier State and Shi'a Islam in the Iranian Revolution," *Theory and Society,* 11, 268.

[2]I have no desire to debate whether the ultimate basis of all political, or even cultural, phenomena is economic. I grant that it is possible to argue that economic causes *ultimately* underlie all the event discussed herein. The point being made here is whether exclusively economic causes *immediately* underlie all cases of revolutionary mobilization. Clearly, I do not think that to be the case.

[3]Samuel Popkin, *The Rational Peasant: The Political Economy of Rural Society in Vietnam* (Berkeley, California: University of California Press, 1979). I do not argue that Popkin's framework exhaustively explains the Iranian case, nor that the two cases — Iran and Vietnam — share more than a handful of pertinent similarities. Rather, I argue that this handful of similarities is powerful circumstantial evidence that culture can condition an environment such that the problem of collective action is more easily overcome.

[4]Certainly egoism is not a necessary condition for rational choice analysis (whether an actor's utility preferences are self-interested or self-disinterested is irrelevant). However, Olson clearly makes the assumption of egoism. See Mancur Olson, *The Logic of Collective Action: Public Goods and the Theory of Groups* (Cambridge, Massachusetts: Harvard University Press, 1971), p. 2.

[5]Ibid. p. 5.

[6]Popkin, *The Rational Peasant,* p. 254.

[7]Ibid. pp. 259-262.

[8]I recognize the shortcoming of analyses which have focused on Tehran, often to the exclusion of equally important provincial centers of revolutionary activity. However, I suggest that strong demographic similarities among the urban poor in Tehran and other major cities compensates for any skewing of my analysis insofar as the social composition of this stratum in most Iranian cities is remarkably homogeneous.

[9]Farhad Kazemi, *Poverty and Revolution in Iran: The Migrant Poor, Urban Marginality and Politics* (New York: New York University Press, 1980).

[10]Mihdi Salamit, et. al., *Ilal-i Muhajirat va Barrisi'y-i Awza-i Farhang-i, Igifsadi, va Ijtima'i-yi Muhajirin-i Mantagih-yi Yakhchiabad* (Tehran: College of Social Work, 1971).

[11]See Gregory Rose, "Velayat-e Fagih and the Recovery of Islamic Identity in the Thought of Ayatollah Khomeini," in Nikki Keddie, ed., *Religion and Politics in Iran: Shi'ism from Quietism to Revolution* (New Haven, Connecticut: Yale University Press, 1983), pp. 166-188.

[12]Popkin, *The Rational Peasant,* p. 255.

[13]Wilfred Cantwell Smith, "Faith as Tasdiq," in Parviz Moreuedge, ed., *Islamic Philosophical Theology* (Albany, New York: State University of New York Press, 1979).

[14]Iranian census-takers systematically excluded potential respondents without permanent addresses and have been accused of underestimating the urban poor population of Tehran by as much as 50%.

[15]In March 1979 I was afforded the opportunity by the Government of the Islamic Republic of Iran to examine confidential reports of the imperial regime's National Security and Intelligence Organization (SAVAK) which repeatedly emphasized the growth of religious consciousness and observance among Tehran's urban poor in the period 1975-1978.

[16]Alexander J. Field, "The Problem with Neoclassical Insititutional Economics: A Critique with Special Reference to North/Thomas Model of pre-1500 Europe, *Explorations in Economic History,* Volume 18, No. 2, 174-198.

[17]Clifford Geertz, *The Interpretation of Cultures* (New York: Basic Books, 1973), p. 14.

Recruitment of Italian Political Terrorists

LEONARD WEINBERG
AND WILLIAM LEE EUBANK

9

I

Understanding the growth of political terrorism has become a central concern expressed in the professional literature. Various techniques have been used to measure the spread of terrorist events both within and between nations.[1] As part of this endeavor analysts have drawn parallels between the spread of contagious diseases and outbreaks of terrorist activities. And naturally enough, given the way in which the situation has been defined, these analysts have sought to prescribe the most appropriate therapies with which to reduce or eliminate the infection.

In view of the way in which the problem has been approached, it is somewhat surprising that more attention has not been focused on the bearers of the contagion: the terrorists themselves. This is not to say that observers of political terrorism have ignored the perpetrators: far from it. The literature abounds with excellent studies of the social and psychological characteristics of these individuals.[2] But these investigations, intended to produce a 'terrorist profile,' seem not to take into account the possibility that different sorts of people might be attracted to terrorism at different stages in the spread of the phenomenon. Do people from the same or similar backgrounds become involved in terrorist operations over the entire life-span of a terrorist organization? Or, does the susceptibility vary among individuals the longer the outbreak is sustained?

Given the enormous attention terrorist activities receive in the mass media, it seems reasonable to believe that individuals who join or form terrorist groups after a terrorist episode has begun would confront a different situation than those who were responsible for its initiation. At a minimum, the circumstances would be altered by virtue of the fact that the latecomers would be aware of the various costs, risks and opportunities surrounding the decision to become the member of a terrorist band. But do changes in circumstances mean changes in the kinds of people who become terrorists? Of course, in any number of countries this question is rendered moot because the authorities succeed in isolating and repressing the terrorist organizations before they can recruit new members from outside the ranks of their founders.

This has not been the case in Italy however. Among the industrialized democracies, Italy has experienced one of the most protracted national episodes of political terrorism. The episode is widely regarded as having begun with the bombing of the National Agricultural Bank of Piazza Fontana in Milan in December 1969 and not to have ended, or even subsided, until the wave of arrests that followed the release of American General

James Dozier from his Red Brigades' kidnappers in 1982. At a reduced level of intensity, the terrorism continues to the present.

In addition to its duration there are several other features of the Italian terrorist experience that are important to call to the reader's attention.[3] First, as distinguished from the long-lived experiences of Northern Ireland and the Basque country of Spain, causes of a nationalist-separatist nature were not significant stimuli for the outbeak of terrorism. Instead, the sources in the Italian case appear to have been predominantly ideological, sources not rooted in the long-standing grievances of a particular ethnic or religious community; that is, groups whose members often may serve as constant pools from which terrorist bands may recruit new adherents. Second, the ideologies that motivated Italian terrorists were not exclusively of leftist origin. In addition to groups animated by revolutionary communist objectives, variously defined, a substantial amount of the violence was the work of formations that derived their inspiration from Fascist or neo-Fascist doctrines.

Another characteristic of the Italian experience concerns the timing of the violence. There was an initial wave of terrorism beginning in 1969 and extending to 1976. By the middle of that year most members of the Red Brigades' 'historic nucleus' as well as most members of the Armed Proletarian Nuclei and Partisan Action Groups, the other major leftist groups, had been arrested. Furthermore, the initial wave of violent neo-Fascist organizations, the New Order, National Vanguard, the National Front and others, had been dissolved by the authorities and many of their leaders, militants and sponsors had met the same fate as their leftist counterparts. In fact, it appeared as if the terrorist episode had come to an end. But this was not to be. Nineteen seventy-seven witnessed the reignition of terrorist violence. New groups on both the Left and Right arose to take the place of the old; in turn, these bands succeeded in recruiting large numbers of new adherents. Further, old groups, notably the Red Brigades, managed to attract a largely new generation(s) of members. What then followed in the next several years was a dramatic escalation in the numbers of terrorist events throughout the country. The style of the violence was also somewhat different. Previously the leftist groups had carried out "exemplary actions" intended to bring their cause to the attention of the working class. In the new phase they began to wage revolutionary "campaigns" against the bourgeois system and to direct their efforts against "the heart of the state." The neo-Fascist groups also changed tactics and exhibited a willingness to attack selected representatives of government authority. Finally, the second spasm of terrorism differed from the initial one by virtue of the political coloration of those groups responsible for committing the bulk of it.[4]

Measured in terms of direction, the first wave of violence was dominated by the neo-Fascists. It was they who were responsible for the majority of violent events, including the massacres at Piazza Fontana as well as those in Brescia and on the express train Italicus both in 1974. The Red Brigades, on the other hand, did not kill their first victim until 1974. Despite the formation of new neo-Fascist groups (e.g., Third Position, Nuclei of

Armed Revolutionaries) after the mid 1970's, it was the revolutionary communist ones that dominated terrorist activities from 1977. There was, in short, a shift from Black to Red.

II

Bearing in mind the above account, the question we intend to address is this: In what ways, if any, did individuals who became involved in terrorist activities before 1977 differ from those whose careers in terrorism began in or followed that year? To answer this question biographical information was obtained concerning 2,512 individuals who were either arrested or for whom warrants were issued for having committed, planned or supported acts of political terrorism between 1970 and the first half of 1984. This information was derived from two national circulation newspapers, *La Stampa* of Turin and *La Repubblica* of Rome, as well as court records (*requisitorie, ordinanze/sentenze* and *sentenze*) from many though not all of the major terrorist trials.[5] The data file taken from these sources does not represent a sample, it is instead a reasonably extensive collection of the Italian terrorist population. The information collected about the terrorists included their gender, communities and regions of birth as well as those of adult residence. Aside from these characteristics, information was also recorded concerning their occupational backgrounds, family relationships and pre-terrorist political involvements. Finally, we noted in what year they were arrested/identified as terrorists, their ages at that time (and for reasons to be made clear later, their ages in 1969), the particular terrorist organization with which they were affiliated and the roles they played inside the groups.

However, the investigators cannot be certain but that either they or their sources failed to locate other individuals whose behavior would warrant inclusion. Further, the possibility exists that a number of individuals whose records appear in the file were, in fact, innocent of the crimes they were alleged to have committed. Last on our list of qualifications is the fact that the careers of some terrorists overlapped the two periods into which we have divided the episode. Some individuals may have begun their involvements before 1977 but only came to the attention of the authorities during or after that year. In most cases, it was possible to correct for this problem based on the person's terrorist group affiliation. That is, if the person was identified as a member of a group like the New Order of the Nuclei of Armed Proletarians, organizations whose operations were largely confined to the first period, the individual was presumed to have begun his/her involvement at that time and assigned a position accordingly. Inevitably though some individuals escaped this procedure. But given the size of the data file, their impact on the overall analysis is not likely to be a very large one.

III

For some observers, Italian terrorism is best understood as a by-product of the "culture of 1968."[6] In 1968 and the "hot autumn" of 1969, Italy experienced a massive explosion of student protest and worker militancy. The events of these years have been defined as an institutional crisis, with existing political, educational and trade union organizations proving unable to contain or channel the rapid mobilization of so many angry citizens. Radical extraparliamentary movements were organized by and for those students, workers and alienated individuals from various walks of life who found existing institutions to have fallen victim to something approaching the iron law of oligarchy. The events of 1968-69 have also been interpreted as a generational rebellion. The young, of neo-Fascist as well as leftist disposition, withdrew their support from or de-authorized a whole array of institutions they perceived as having become dominated by gerontocratic leaderships.

This institutional crisis or generational rebellion had profound consequences on the development of political terrorism. One interpretation has it that some individuals, those who organized the Red Brigades' for example, initiated terrorist activities after brief transitional exposures to the extraparliamentary movements. For other future leftist terrorists the impact of 1968-69 was delayed. After years of membership in extraparliamentary movements like Worker Power and Continuous Struggle, these individuals turned to terrorism after the collapse of the New Left in the 1976 national elections, elections which also resulted in a failure to remove the hated Christian Democratics from control of the national government. As the radicals saw it, years of struggle by the movements had come to nothing. The only way to unblock the Italian political system and achieve their revolutionary objectives was through use of political violence. The Communist party, a likely alternative, was unable to integrate the revolutionaries; in 1976 it was pursuing an historic compromise with the Christian Democrats, a policy of reformism and working class betrayal from their perspective.

This commentary suggests an understanding of the terrorist phenomenon through what amounts to a "big bang" theory. The events of 1968-69 were a formative experience for a generation of young Italians. The effects, immediate for some long-term for others, were to provide an impetus for involvement in terrorism. To become a terrorist one had to be touched directly by the events of 1968-69.

Although this was no doubt true for some, in general the data do not support this interpretation (see Table 1). Of the 2,512 individuals in our terrorist population, 46 per cent were under the age of 16 in 1969, and 18 per cent were less than 11 years old when the upheaval occurred. In other words, these were people too young to have taken a direct part in the turbulent events of these years.

TABLE 1
Age Distribution of Italian Terrorists in 1969

Age	Number of Terrorists	(Per Cent)
1 to 5	17	(1)
6 to 10	417	(17)
11 to 15	732	(29)
16 to 20	556	(22)
21 to 25	295	(12)
26 to 30	131	(5)
31 to 35	56	(2)
36 to 40	42	(2)
41 to 45	31	(1)
46 to 50	16	(1)
51 and above	219	(9)
	N = 2,512	(100)

Even if we confine the analysis to left-wing terrorists, the segment of the population really intended to be covered by this interpretation, the outcome is not altered. In fact, the left-wing terrorists were actually younger in 1969 than were the neo-Fascists. Of the 1,763 leftists in the study, 853 (or 64 per cent) were under 16. Furthermore, if 1968-69 was crucial in the making of terrorists, we would expect that over time their ages would increase as they were apprehended or identified by the authorities. Yet this is not true either. The terrorists identified in 1977 and after were significantly younger than those whose involvements were reported during the first period.

If participation in the events of 1968-69 was not an indispensable ingredient in the decision to embark on a career as a terrorist, it would seem likely that some process of cultural or ideological transmission was at work. If it was not the same individuals sharing the same experiences, then perhaps the post 1976 terrorists became susceptible to the contagion as the result of exposure to the same social climate and institutional setting as gave rise to the first wave.

We sought to deal with this issue by dividing our population into those individuals who were identified as terrorists before 1977 and those who received the designation in 1977 and after. The differences between the two groups are summarized in Table 2.

TABLE 2
Differences Between Early (1970-1976)
and Late (1977-1984) Italian Terrorists

Characteristic	2A: Sex		
	Male	Female	
Early	449 (23.8)*	50 (11.2)	499
Late	1441 (76.2)	395 (88.8)	1836
	1890	445	

$X^2 = 32.86$ prob. $\leq$ .001   phi = .12

* Percentages in parenthesis are column percents.

85

2B: Birthplace
(region)

	North	Center	Rome	South	Foreign Born	
Early	156 (31.0)	50 (34.0)	37 (16.7)	58 (18.7)	5 (11.9)	306
Late	348 (69.0)	97 (66.0)	184 (83.3)	252 (81.3)	37 (88.1)	918
	504	147	221	310	42	1224

$X^2 = 34.31$ prob. $\leq$ .001   tau b = .13

2C: Birthplace
(size of community)

	Small	Medium	Big City	Foreign Born	
Early	86 (19.5)	109 (28.2)	119 (24.0)	5 (11.9)	319
Late	354 (80.5)	277 (71.8)	377 (76.0)	37 (88.1)	1054
	440	386	496	42	1364

$X^2 = 11.88$ prob. $\leq$ .001   tau b = -.02

2D: Place of Residence
(region)

	North	Center	Rome	South	Foreign Born	
Early	273 (22.6)*	60 (26.1)	80 (14.0)	57 (22.5)	1 (33.3)	471
Late	935 (77.4)	170 (73.9)	492 (86.0)	196 (77.5)	2 (66.7)	1795
	1208	230	572	253	3	2266

$X^2 = 23.15$ prob. $\leq$ .001   tau b = .047

2E: Place of Residence
(size of community)

	Small	Medium	Big City	Foreign Born	
Early	52 (21.7)	136 (26.1)	285 (18.9)	1 (33.3)	474
Late	188 (78.3)	386 (73.9)	1226 (81.1)	2 (66.7)	1802
	240	522	1226	3	2276

$X^2 = 12.57$ prob. $\leq$ .006   tau b = .058

2F: Family Relationship to Other Terrorists

	Yes	No	
Early	51 (16.7)	443 (21.9)	494
Late	254 (83.3)	1582 (78.1)	1836
	305	2025	2330

$X^2 = 3.91$ prob. $\leq$ .04   phi = .043

2G: Type of Family Relationship

	Marital	Sibling	Parental	Other	
Early	16 (11.8)*	26 (18.7)	5 (41.7)	4 (22.2)	51
Late	120 (88.2)	113 (81.3)	7 (58.3)	14 (77.8)	254
	136	139	12	18	305

$X^2 = 8.54$ prob. $\leq$ .036   tau b = -.132

* Percentages in parenthesis are column percents.

2H: Prior Political Party Affiliation

	Left	Center	Right	
Early	30 (30.2)	3 (75.0)	63 (73.3)	85
Late	44 (69.8)	1 (25.0)	23 (26.7)	68
	63	4	86	153

X^2 = 27.98   prob. ≤ .001

2I: Extraparliamentary Movement Affiliation

	Left	Right	
Early	39 (11.4)	149 (85.6)	188
Late	302 (88.6)	25 (14.4)	327
	341	174	

X^2 = 270.43   prob. ≤ .001   phi = .723

2J: Age at Time of Identification

	15 to 19	20 to 24	25 to 29	30 to 34	35 to 39	40 to 44	45 to 49	50 and above	
Early	27 (17.6)*	150 (19.7)	117 (18.5)	62 (18.7)	31 (24.8)	24 (41.4)	22 (68.8)	34 (72.3)	467
Late	126 (82.4)	611 (80.3)	514 (81.5)	269 (81.3)	94 (75.2)	34 (58.6)	10 (31.3)	13 (27.7)	1671
	153	761	631	331	125	58	32	47	2138

X^2 = 134.56   prob. ≤ .00   tau b = -.102

2K: Occupation

	Subproletariate	Student	Worker	Police Military	White Collar Clerk	Shopkeeper Salesman Artisan	Teacher	Free Professional	Industrialist Business Manager	Housewife	
Early	11 (17.5)	74 (21.1)	45 (12.7)	27 (52.9)	25 (11.5)	27 (46.6)	14 (11.3)	38 (39.6)	23 (65.7)	1 (9.1)	285
Late	52 (82.5)	277 (78.9)	310 (87.3)	24 (47.1)	193 (88.5)	31 (53.4)	110 (88.7)	58 (60.4)	12 (34.3)	10 (90.9)	1077
	63	351	355	51	218	58	124	96	35	11	1362

X^2 = 151.97   prob. ≤ .00   tau b = -.085

2L: Role in Terrorist Group

	Supporter	Regular	Leader	
Early	22 (4.7)	379 (23.5)	94 (37.3)	495
Late	443 (95.3)	1235 (76.5)	158 (62.7)	1836
	465	1614	252	2331

X^2 = 119.48   prob. ≤ .00   tau b = -.218

---

* Percentages in parenthesis are column percents.

The principal understanding to be derived from these results is that there occurred an expansion of terrorism to wider segments of Italian society as the episode progressed. Instead of a repetitive process with the new generation(s) of terrorists simply recapitulating the institutional and social backgrounds of the early ones, in general, the evidence suggests that terrorist groups were able to broaden, not merely deepen, their appeal the longer the episode continued.

Let us be more specific. While the early terrorists were overwhelmingly male, the second wave contained a significant contingent of women. If we examine the question of where the terrorists came from by looking at their places of birth, compared to the first one, the second generation over-represents people who were born in smaller communities (under 100,000) as well as in Rome, southern Italy and abroad. Geographically it appears as if the terrorists' roots descend from the northern and central parts of the country to the south and out from the big cities (over 1 million) to smaller towns the longer the violence persists. However, when we compare the two groups not by their places of birth but by their places of adult residence, some interesting changes occur. Here the second generation appears somewhat less geographically dispersed than the first. This is true especially of the size of the communities in which the terrorists had become resident prior to beginning their careers in political violence. The latecomers were more likely to have lived in the big cities of Rome, Turin, Genoa, Milan and Naples than their predecessors. It may very well be the case then that as a group the later terrorists were more geographically mobile, more likely to have been newcomers to the big cities than members of the initial wave. Whatever terrorist infection got transmitted from one generation to the next seems to have involved a passage from longer to shorter term residents of Italy's major metropolitan areas.

Correlatively, the occupational backgrounds of the terrorists seem to exhibit a process of expansion. In general, though not without qualification, the pattern is one of a spread from the upper strata of Italian society to the lower. Higher proportions of the early terrorists than the later came from upper status positions as business managers, industrialists and the free professions (law, medicine, architecture, journalism). The first group was also composed disproportionately of individuals with lower middle class occupational experiences as shopkeepers, salesmen and artisans as well as police and military officers. On the other hand, the latecomers were over-represented among manual workers and white collar clerks, and to a lesser extent of subproletarians (e.g., criminals, ex-convicts, prostitutes). Students from universities and secondary schools make a relatively constant and large contribution to the terrorists' ranks. Although the level of student involvement remains roughly the same in the two periods, the same cannot be said for their teachers. The representation of university and secondary school instructors increases substantially from 1977 forward.

If we treat these data somewhat differently and regard as "intellectuals" (that is people who spend a fair amount of their working time dealing with abstract ideas) students, teachers and free professionals, the consequence is that their contribution to terrorist activities appears both high and constant. What becomes variable between the two periods is the representation of individuals with backgrounds in business and labor. In the first period business is over-represented while in the second labor is.

For some of the individuals in the population, the decision to become a terrorist seems to have been a matter of family choice. Slightly over 13 per cent of the terrorists were related to one another. This phenomenon was more prevalent among the second wave than the first, however. In this connection, it is the incidence of the marital relationship that really changes from the first to the second periods. Although we cannot be sure, the greater prevalence of married couples to be found among the later adherents to terrorist groups may have been the consequence of husbands encouraging their wives to join, a particularly intimate form of contagion.

The two segments of our population also appear to have had somewhat different kinds of pre-terrorist political experiences. Prior membership in a conventional political party was more common among early than later terrorists. Conversely, the latter were more likely to have been members of the extraparliamentary movements. The biographical records are incomplete but we may at least speculate that over time terrorism spread from individuals who were more likely to have had experiences in conventional party political life to those whose involvements were more likely confined to the violence supportive extraparliamentary movements or to individuals with no reported preterrorist political experiences.

Finally, the early and late terrorists are distinguishable on the basis of the roles they played once inside terrorist organizations. Here the prevalence of individuals identified as "supporters," those who furnished logistical and other forms of assistance, increased dramatically among the late adherents. This finding may be the result of the development of a more complex organizational structure articulated by terrorist groups after 1976 as well as an increase in their recruitment of and appeal to part-timers, individuals holding regular jobs whose commitments to the terrorist enterprise were likely less intense than persons identified as "regulars" or "leaders" in the newspaper accounts and court records.

At this stage of the analysis the evidence points to an understanding of Italian terrorism that emphasizes its diffusion to progressively broader segments of the population. There appear to have been changes of various kinds in the geographic, institutional and social settings from which the terrorists emerged. But to what extent were these changes simply an artifact of the differential representation of leftist and neo-Fascist terrorists in the two periods with which we are concerned? As may be seen by looking at Table 3, a majority of pre-1977 terrorists were neo-Fascists while the great preponderance of the later adherents were leftists. It may very well be that the early/late distinctions we have observed were more a product of the different political composition of the two groups than they were the time periods during which these individuals engaged in terrorist activities.

TABLE 3
Distribution of Terrorists
by Period and Political Orientation

	Early	Late	
Right	293	279	572
Left	206	1557	1763
	499	1836	2335

N = 2335

In order to determine whether or not this is the case we partitioned our population into the following four categories: early right, late right, early left and late left. The relevant questions then became: Were the early neo-Fascists different from the late ones? And, were there any ways in which the early leftists differed from their political successors?

In attempting to answer the first question let us begin with the negative findings. First, there was no significant difference among the neo-Fascists concerning their occupational backgrounds. In both periods they tended to come from the same lower middle and upper middle class sectors of Italian society. In addition, they tended to be drawn from the same right-wing political milieu. There were few neo-Fascists in either period who drifted into terrorism after previous experiences with political parties at the center or left or in the extraparliamentary left movements. On the other hand, there were considerably fewer late neo-Fascists who were reported to have had either right-wing or extraparliamentary involvements before their ties to the terrorist groups developed. Lastly, the late neo-Fascists were no more or less likely to have been related to one another than the first collection.

If we focus on those variables (see Table 4) that exhibit differences between early and late neo-Fascists, the case for a process of expansion becomes far more ambiguous than it does for the general terrorist population. It is true that the later neo-Fascists were substantially younger than the earlier group. The representation of women increases, although it is never very high among the neo-Fascists. Also, the proportion of "supporters" relative to "regulars" and "leaders" grows in the second wave. Yet when we look at their places of birth and adult residence, the case for the diffusion of neo-Fascist terrorism by expansion weakens. Measured both in terms of where they were born and resided the early neo-Fascists were a more geographically dispersed collection of people than the later ones.

TABLE 4
Differences Between Early (1970-1976)
and Late (1977-1984) Neo-Fascist Terrorists

Characteristics	Early to Late Change
Sex	late more female
	$x^2 = 9.82$, 1 df, $p \le .002$, phi $= .138$
Age	late younger
	$x^2 = 91.92$, 7 df, $p \le .001$, $s_b = -.363$
Place of Birth (region)	late more Rome less North and Center
	$x^2 = 108.19$, 4 df, $p \le .001$, $\vartheta = .471$
Place of Birth (size of community)	late more big city less small town and medium-sized cities
	$x^2 = 30.83$, 3 df, $p \le .01$, $s_b = .251$
Place of Residence (region)	late more Rome less North and Center
	$x^2 = 218.76$, 4 df, $p \le .001$, $\vartheta = .618$
Place of Residence (size of community)	late more big city less small town and medium-sized city
	$x^2 = 81.53$, 3 df, $p \le .001$, $\vartheta = .344$
Role in Organization	late more supporters less regulars and leaders
	$x^2 = 132.20$, 2 df, $p \le .001$, $s_b = -.438$

After the mid-1970's the neo-Fascists were a waning force. Their leaders' plans to stimulate a coup d'etat against the Italian regime, with the collaboration of well-wishers in the police and military establishments, had been uncovered and defeated.[7] The number of terrorist events for which they were responsible declined. In a sense our findings reflect this decline. Geographically we witness a contraction or concentration rather than a diffusion of neo-Fascist terrorism between the two time periods. As a group the late neo-Fascists are more urbanized and Rome-centered than the early ones. However, when we consider the matter from a social or inter-personal perspective, there is some evidence of spread, if not in terms of occupational background then at least as reflected by their ages, gender and level of involvement in their respective terrorist organizations.

While neo-Fascist terrorism may have been waning in the second period, left-wing terrorism was expanding. As measured by the number of violent events and in the number of adherents included in our population, terrorism from the left experienced considerable growth. Logically then we might expect this growth to be reflected in a wider diffusion process than was true for the neo-Fascists.

In some respects (see Table 5) the ways in which the growth of left-wing terrorism manifested itself in the changing characteristics of the terrorists was not very different than the early to late changes in the makeup of the declining neo-Fascist formations. As with the latter, the second generation(s) of leftists was younger than the first. It was also more heavily composed of "supporters." In addition, the proportion of adherents identified as playing leadership roles in the groups declined compared to the "regulars" and "supporters." Also, a smaller percentage of the late than the early leftists were reported to have had prior memberships in political parties.

TABLE 5
Differences Between Early (1970-1976)
and Late (1977-1984) Left-Wing Terrorists

Characteristic	Early to Late Change
Age	late younger $x^2 = 218.15$, 10 df, $p \leq .001$, $^5b = -.218$
Place of Residence (region)	late more Center and Rome less South $x^2 = 15.61$, 4 df, $p \leq .004$, $_9 = 0.0$
Nature of Family Relationship	late more marital $x^2 = 8.94$, 3 df, $p \leq .03$, $^5b = .058$
Occupation	late more workers, clerks, teachers less students, free professionals and subproletarians $x^2 = 25.04$, 8 df, $p \leq .003$, $^5b = .023$
Previous Political Experience	late more extraparliamentary movement less political party membership $x^2 = 14.23$, 1 df, $p \leq .001$, $^5b = -.251$
Role in Organization	late more supporters $x^2 = 30.57$, 2 df, $p \leq .001$, $^5b = -.127$

There were some ways in which the changes among leftists were unlike those exhibited by the neo-Fascists. The occupational backgrounds of the leftists are significantly different. Here there are noticeable declines in the proportions of terrorists identified as free professionals and subproletarians as well as a more modest decline in the representation of students. The proportions of manual workers, white collar clerks and teachers increases. The effect of these changes though is hardly like that of the overall terrorist population shown earlier. While it is true that the second period leftist organizations were more successful in recruiting manual workers than the first, the relatively clear pattern of terrorism spreading from high to low status in the Italian occupational structure now becomes unclear. This pattern now seems to have been more a product of the different mixes of neo-Fascists and leftists found in the two periods. The neo-Fascists, early and late, tended to come from higher status backgrounds than the leftists taken as a whole.

When we consider the issue from a geographic perspective, we are unable to discern any significant changes in the locations in which the leftists were born. Late leftists were no more or less likely to have been born in the South or smaller communities, for example, than their predecessors. There is, however, a noticeable early-to-late shift in their places of residence, with the second generation more likely to be found in the central regions and Rome. The representation of terrorists from the heavily industrialized northern regions remains very high over both periods. The case for a diffusion of terrorism by expansion is attenuated by the fact that there are proportionately fewer residents of the South among the late leftists and there are no significant differences between the two groups related to the size of the communities in which they were resident.

So far as the terrorists' gender is concerned, somewhat surprisingly the late leftists did not show a statistically significant increase in female representation as against the early contingent. There is a shift, however, in the kinds of women who appear during the second period. The data suggest an increase in the proportion of married women who participated in the left-wing groups. Furthermore, second generation women were more likely to play leadership roles in these groups than were women who joined the earlier formations.[8]

IV

It is apparent now that some of the diffusion effects we reported earlier in the analysis were the result of the differing mixes of neo-Fascists and left-wing revolutionaries present in the two periods of Italy's terrorist episode. The ideologies seem to attract rather different kinds of people to terrorism. Yet there were some differences that were sustained despite the political distinction. If we are willing to conceive the diffusion of terrorism as the result of (1) expansion, its spread to progressively wider segments of the population, and (2) contagion, the spread of the infection more deeply within the same population segments, our findings may be summarized in the following Table 6.

TABLE 6
The Diffusion of Terrorism

Expansion for Left and Right	*Expansion for Left Only*
age, prior political experience, place of residence (Rome) and role in organization	Occupation, place of residence (central regions) family relationship
Expansion for Right Only	*Contagion for Left and Right ±*
sex (more female, place of birth (region and size of community), place of residence (size of community)	none
Contagion for Left Only	*Contagion for Right Only*
sex, place of birth (region and size of community)	occupation

The existence of substantively significant differences is the basis for the classification displayed in Table 6. If such differences were found between the characteristics of early and late terrorists, then these characteristics were noted as having spread by expansion. Some of the differences were common to both neo-Fascists and leftists, others were specific to one or the other. They were classified accordingly. If, on the other hand, no meaningful differences were found between the characteristics'of neo-Fascist and leftist terrorists active in the two periods, the diffusion was conceived to be the product of a contagion effect, with the early terrorists infecting the late. The classification reflects this concept as well.

There were several characteristics of the terrorist population which spread through expansion between the two periods and were common to rightists and leftists alike. Over time the terrorists tended to become younger, less politically experienced and more marginally committed to the groups with which they were affiliated. They were also more likely to be residents of Rome the longer the episode continued. All the other characteristics classified as either expansion or contagion related were ones distinct to the neo-Fascists or the leftist revolutionaries. And since those differences were discussed earlier, we will not repeat them here.

The findings lead us to conclude that terrorism in Italy spread as the result of both expansion and contagion. In the absence of interviews with a sample of individuals included in the terrorist population, we cannot specify precisely how these components worked in the process of terrorist recruitment. We can, of course, engage in speculation.

One thought that comes to mind is that Italy went through a new crisis in 1976-77, one separable from that of 1968-69. While the latter was of an institutional or generational nature, the former involved problems that had to do with high rates of unemployment and inflation. And as in the first crisis so too in the second, there was a substantial amount of mass street agitation accompanied by accusations of governmental and party political ineptitude. It is conceivable that younger and less politically involved segments of the population largely unaffected by the first crisis were engaged by the second. Aware of terrorism as part of the repertoire of techniques available for the expression of political grievances, an awareness derived from the 1969-76 period, they became susceptable to its use.

We might also speculate that terrorism spread by contagion was the result of exposure to the same social and institutional stimuli, the same living and working environments from which the early terrorists had already been recruited. The FIAT Mirafiori automobile plant in Turin and the universities of Padua and Rome are obvious examples. Concomitantly, it may be the result of exposure to the same sorts of life experiences as already gave rise to terrorist involvements that heighten the susceptibility. This element is probably not missing in the spread of terrorism by expansion either. Yet in this context our suspicion is that the role of the mass media in making people aware of and attracting them to terrorist activities is likely to play a greater role in its cultivation.

Finally, it would be interesting to know if the characteristics we have detected concerning Italy's protracted terrorist experience were unique to that country, or if similar findings might result from investigations conducted elsewhere.

Notes

[1]See, for example, E. Heyman and E. Mickolus, "Imitation by Terrorists: Quantitative Approaches to the Study of Diffusion Patterns in Transnational Terrorism," in Yonah Alexander and J. Gleason, eds., *Behavioral and Quantitative Perspectives on Terrorism* (New York: Pergamon Press, 1981), pp. 175-225. and

L. Hamilton and J. Hamilton, "Dynamics of Terrorism," *International Studies Quarterly,* vol 27 (1983), 39-54.

[2]See, for example, C. Russell and B. Miller, "Profile of a Terrorist," in L. Freedman and Y. Alexander, eds., *Perspectives on Terrorism* (Wilmington: Scholarly Resources, 1983), pp. 45-60.

[3]G. Pasquino, "Differenze e Somiglianze: per Una Ricerca sul Terrorismo Italiano," in D. della Porta and G. Pasquino, eds., *Terrorismo e Violenza Politica* (Bologna: Il Mulino, 1983), pp. 237-263.

[4]D. della Porta and M. Rossi, *I Terrorismi in Italia tra il 1969 e il 1982* (Bologna: Istituto Cattaneo, 1983), pp. 5-14.

[5]In addition to the newspapers biographical information was obtained from the following court records: For the Red Brigades, Front Line, Autonomia and related left-wing groups, Giudice Istruttore, Francesco Amato, *Ordinanza/Sentenza* N/1067/79, Tribunale di Roma; Giudice Istruttore, *Sentenza/Ordinanza* 231/83, Tribunale Civile E. Penale di Milano; Giudice Istruttore *Ordinanza N228/81, Tribunale Civile E. Panale di Milano; Publicco Ministero, Requisitoria* N. 921/80F, Procura Della Repubblica in Milano; Giudice Istruttore, Ferdinando Imposimato, *Odinanza/Sentenza* N54/80A. Tribunale di Roma; Giudice Istruttore, *Odinanza/Sentenza* 490/81F, Tribunale Civile E. Penale di Milano; Corete D'Assisse Di Apo ello Di Torino, *Sentenza* of January 24, 1983, N 2/83; Corte D'Assise D'Apello Di Milano, *Sentenza* of April 9, 1981 N 7/80; Corte D'Assise di Firenze, *Sentenza* of April 24, 1983. For the neo-Fascist groups, Third Position, National Revolutionary Front and We Build the Action, the following court records were obtained: Giudice Istruttore, Luigi gennaro, *Ordinanza/Sentenza* N 2736/80A, Tribunale di Roma; Corte D'Assise di Appello di Firenze, *Sentenza* of December 12, 1978; Corte D'Assise di Appello di Firenze, *Sentenza* of April 9, 1976 and *Sentenza* of November 11, 1977.

[6]A Ventura, "Il Problema delle Origini del Terrorismo di Sinistra," in D. della Porta, ed., *Terrorismi in Italia* (Bologna: Il Mulino, 1985), pp. 75-152.

[7]F. Ferraresi, "La Destra Eversiva," in F. Ferraresi, ed., *La Destra Radicale* (Milan: Feltrinelli, 1984), pp. 54-118.

[8]L. Weinberg and W. Eubank, "Italian Women Terrorists," presented to the Annual Meeting of the Western Social Science Association, Fort Worth, March, 1985.

Alienation: The Case of Catholics in Northern Ireland

10

EDWARD P. MOXON- BROWNE

The word 'alienation' carries a number of intrinsic connotations that are useful when examining a case of political alienation. For Marx, the estrangement of the individual from himself was to be remedied by abolition of private property so that the plight of the individual worker, forced to be simply the means to an economic end, might be shortcircuited. Freud saw the individual estranged from himself by living up to the expectations of others so that (as Marcuse was later to point out) the individual was no longer the originator of his own acts; he was no longer his true self. He lost interest in life because it was not he who was living it.

Clearly, when we are talking about alienation of the Catholic community in Northern Ireland, we are using the term at a more superficial level. However, the historical and socio-psychological antecedents of the term are valuable adjuncts to the specifically political analysis. The alienated citizen is often apathetic because he is not recognized for what he is; and his identity may, at best, be ignored or, at worst, be denigrated. Political lassitude follows logically from a political identity being ghettoised into a backwater far removed from mainstream political life. A dictionary definition of 'alienation' will mention being 'estranged,' 'foreign in nature,' and 'belonging to another place, person or family, especially to a foreign nation or allegiance.'[1] Such a definition usefully bridges the gap between the psychological ('estranged') aspect of the term and the political ('Belonging to a foreign nation or allegiance') dimension. This coupling of two aspects of alienation are especially pertinent when we consider the Catholic minority in Northern Ireland.

In a political context the term alienation denotes the sense of being or feeling, foreign. The alienated group is one that feels foreign although it resides within the state; it feels that it does not fully belong to the wider society and often withdraws into itself and becomes increasingly aware of its separate identity. Such a group is often a numerical minority but it need not be so. The crucial attributes are that it sees itself as being subordinate or marginal to the dominant political culture. Thus Blacks in South Africa, although numerically a majority, are best analyzed as a minority, and an alienated minority within the South African state. Most alienated groups, however, are, numerically speaking, minority groups in a larger society, e.g. the Tamils of Sri Lanka, the Jews of the Soviet Union, or the Sikhs in India.

The word 'alienation' has recently become a prominent weapon in the battle of words between politicians in Britain and Ireland when referring to the position of the Catholic community in Northern Ireland. The New Ireland Forum Report[2] ascribed the impasse in Northern Ireland to the 'alienation of nationalists in Northern Ireland from political and civil institutions, from the security forces and from the manner of application of the law.' The theme seemed to have struck a sympathetic chord when the Secretary of State for Northern Ireland, in a speech in July 1984, stressed the importance of finding mechanisms through which the distinct national identity of Catholics could be expressed. More recently, after the Anglo-Irish summit, the communique spoke of the need to cater for the separate identity and aspirations of the minority. However, more recently still, (November 1984) both the British Prime Minister (Mrs. Thatcher) and the new Northern Ireland Secretary (Mr. Hurd) publicly deplored the use of the word alienation implying that it was both an exaggeration and inaccurate. In response to those statements there has been no shortage of spokesmen for the Catholic community indicating the extent of the alienation they perceive among their coreligionists. For example, the Bishop of Down and Connor, whose diocese includes Belfast, wrote in late November of 1984:

> It has been claimed this week, even at Prime Ministerial and Secretary of State level, that the degree of alienation has been exaggerated, perhaps even that the term itself if inappropriate. Living in day to day contact with the situation as I do, I have to assert quite categorically that the alienation in the nationalist community is real, it is profound, it is increasing, it is spreading to more and more sectors of that community.[3]

Since there appears to be wide disagreement between leading actors in the Northern Ireland situation as to whether and, if so how much, alienation is experienced by the Catholic community, it is timely for some kind of analysis to be carried out. Otherwise, there is a danger that the word alienation will simply become a rhetorical device for political point scoring. Already, in fact, some spokesmen for the majority Protestant community have pointed to the alienation that they feel, for example, at policemen being gunned down in the streets. This sort of counter charge, based as it undoubtedly is on a real sense of grievance, risks devaluing the intrinsic worth of 'alienation' as a political concept. The experience of alienation, claimed by the Catholic community has important policy implications. The state must, presumably, react to alienation if it perceives it as being widespread. To ignore alienation, or to wish it away by pretending it is not there, could lead to policies that are not simply unhelpful, but actually counter-productive.

In this paper, the term alienation will be operationalized along a continuum ranging from abstentionism at one extreme to support for violence against the state, at the other. The actual components of alienation that are being examined here are (in ascending order of gravity):

(a) identification with a national ethos distinct from the national ethos of the majority

(b) support for policies involving another state in policy-making; and, at the same time, abstentionism from the political process within the state

(c) lack of support for, and hostility to, the judicial system, the forces of law and order, and the penal system of the state

(d) support for political parties that condone violence as a means of effecting political change; support for paramilitary groups; support for violence to overthrow the state.

Fortunately for the social scientist, there are numerous mass opinion surveys in Northern Ireland that can be used to facilitate a reasonably accurate measurement of the four components of alienation outlined above. Mass opinion surveys can be buttressed by election results and the policy programmes of political parties. From such measurement, a number of hypotheses suggest themselves:

(a) the Catholic community experiences alienation to a greater or lesser degree in terms of the above components

(b) alienation is, however, experienced in varying degrees of severity; and socioeconomic status, age and political party affiliation will be variables strongly associated with experience of alienation

(c) tensions within the Catholic community are attributable not so much to the differential experience of alienation, but to the means of overcoming it

Our analysis will proceed in three steps. First, we will place the Catholic community in its demographic context. Second, in the main body of the paper, we will analyse each of the four components of alienation in terms of mass opinion survey evidence. Thirdly, we will reappraise each of our hypotheses in the light of the evidence that has been adduced, and conclude with an assessment of the extent to which they can be confirmed or rejected.

The Catholic community

The national population census in the United Kingdom is conducted once every ten years. The most recent census (1981) is not a completely reliable statement of the religious complexion of the Northern Ireland population because there was a considerable resistance (especially among Catholics) to the question on the religion of the respondent and, to a lesser extent, to filling out the census form at all. It has been estimated that 22% of the total population in Northern Ireland failed to state their religion either because they refused to answer the relevant question or because they refused to fill in a form. This short-fall is reckoned to be about twice as great as that of the previous census in 1971.[4] This resistance to the census can itself be regarded as a symptom of alienation in the Catholic community: census forms were burnt in public on the streets, and a female census enumerator was shot dead.

As part of its task of ensuring that employment patterns reflect the local denominational structure of the population, the Fair Employment Agency in Northern Ireland undertook a study to ascertain, more accurately than the 1981 census, the size of the Catholic community.[5] This Report made use of school registers, parochial records, and government-sponsored household surveys. The Report, published in 1985, concluded that the

Catholic share of the total population (1,562,200) was 39.1% in 1981, compared with 34% as reported in the 1981 census (and 31% in the 1971 census). The Catholic community is relatively youthful: 46% of the under-15's in the Province were Catholic, and 36% of the adults. Moreover, the fertility rate remains higher among Catholics than Protestants (the ratio of children to married women for Catholics and Protestants is 2.57 and 1.6 respectively). Of the 26 local government districts in Northern Ireland, eight have a majority of Catholic adults, but twelve have a majority of Catholic schoolchildren. Given the age profile of the Catholic community, and its relatively higher fertility rate, it has been suggested that the minority in Northern Ireland could become a majority early in the next century. If we extrapolate present reproductive differentials between the two communities, and assume no emigration, it is possible to foresee the Catholic community becoming a majority of the voting-age population by the year 2025.[6]

The purpose of the foregoing remarks is to emphasize that the Catholic minority in Northern Ireland is (a) a very large minority and (b) increasing in size both relatively and absolutely. This has important repercussions for our discussion of alienation among Catholics. It is easier for a group that constitutes, say, 5% of the total population (e.g. Protestants in the Republic of Ireland), to accept that its political leverage or access to economic resources may be marginal in terms of the national total. It is much more difficult for a minority constituting 40% of the population to accept inferior treatment in economic, political or judicial domains. As the relative size of the Catholic community increases, the pressure on the national government in London to accommodate these increased demands (especially when expectations are higher) will increase *pari passu*.

On this 'bedrock of alienation' lies a substructure of perceived relative deprivation vis-a-vis the chosen reference group i.e. the Protestant majority. In the political sphere, a high degree of overlap[7] between religious affiliation and party identification means that the Catholic minority parties have been effectively excluded from policy-making since 1922. The refusal of the Protestant majority parties to countenance any form of 'partnership' or 'consociationalism'[8] as a formula for giving Catholics access to real political power, has alienated the two main Catholic parties from the political process. This marginality of the Catholic community to the political process is compounded by its marginality in other key state agencies e.g. the police (where Catholic participation is about 10%); the Civil Service (where a recent report[9] showed that 'Roman Catholics are not adequately represented at the key policy-making levels'); and in the judiciary where only three out of twenty judges are Catholics.

More immediate, perhaps, is the marginality of the Catholic community to the region's economic life. Aunger[10] has shown that 'there is a marked tendency for Protestants to dominate the upper occupational classes while Catholics are found predominantly in the lower classes.' Aunger also found that Catholics are two and a half times more likely to be unemployed than Protestants. In his 1978 mass opinion survey, Moxon-Browne found 7% of his Protestant respondents and 14% of his Catholic respondents without jobs.[11] Catholic males are particularly badly affected. They constitute less than 21% of the economically active population, but 44% of the unemployed. Within work contexts, Protestants are more likely to be found in supervisory roles or high status positions than are Catholics. Thus in the medical sector, for example, 21% of doctors are Catholic, but 43% of nurses. In education, Catholics have 15% of the administrative positions but 39% of those in teaching. The rather high proportion of Catholics in non-manual occupations is attributed by Aunger to the need of the Catholic community to 'service' itself. Thus teachers and clergymen account for one-third of Catholic non-manual occupations while the equivalent figure for the Protestant community is 19%. In a highly segregated society, the existence of a Catholic middle class, whose primary role is to cater to the needs of its own community, does little to mitigate the marginality of Catholics in the economy generally.

The components of 'alienation'

We turn now to consider the four components of Catholic alienation mentioned earlier. The first of these was 'identification with a national ethos distinct from the national ethos of the majority.' The birth of Northern Ireland as a political entity was destined to guarantee a bifurcated sense of national identity within its boundaries. Ireland had never been absorbed politically or culturally into the United Kingdom as effectively as Scotland or Wales. In 1920, Northern Ireland might have left the United Kingdom had it not been for the determination of a majority of its inhabitants to remain part of a British state. The resulting constitutional formula was a messy compromise (a devolved government) that pleased no-one. Catholics felt aggrieved that they were now 'trapped' in a 'Protestant state;' the Protestants felt aggrieved that their region was now to be governed at one remove from London; and the British government was less than pleased at being unable to offload responsibility for the region onto a government in Dublin.

The legacy of this settlement was that national identity became a divisive concept. Broadly speaking, Catholics tended to look south to the government in Dublin as the appropriate focus for their Irish national identity. Protestants continued to look towards London as the focus for their British identity. Politics within the region became rooted in the constitutional question: most Catholics persisted in feeling that their identity could not be given true expression except in an all-Ireland state (and this aspiration was given some legitimacy by the Constitutional claim to the territory of Northern Ireland by the Republic of Ireland). Most Protestants persisted in their fear that their British identity would be in jeopardy if Irish unity was ever achieved, and in their belief that their economic, political and cultural interests could only be safeguarded within a British state.

Opinion survey evidence suggests that Catholics are surer of their national identity than are Protestants. When asked to indicate their national 'label,' Catholics will overwhelmingly reply 'Irish' while Protestants may say 'Ulster' or 'British.' Rose argues that Protestants national identity is partly based on a negative reaction to being thought of as 'Irish:' they may be vague about what they are, but they are sure about what they are not. This is confirmed in Rose's finding that most Irish people attribute their nationality to being 'born and bred' (93% of the group) while 53% of those who see themselves as British attribute this to being 'under British rule' (an inherently less secure basis for national allegiance).[12]

In Table 1, we can see the extent to which national identity follows religious lines in Northern Ireland. We can also see that, in the ten-year period (1968-78), being British (and not being Irish) has become more important for Protestants.

TABLE 1
Northern Identity in Northern Ireland: 1968 and 1978

Question: Which of these terms best describes the way you usually think of yourself? British, Irish, Ulster, Sometimes British, Sometimes Irish, Anglo-Irish, Other?

	Catholics %		Protestants %	
	1968	1978	1968	1978
British	15	15	39	67
Irish	76	69	20	8
Ulster	5	6	32	20

N.B. Percentages are rounded to the nearest digit. Responses for 'British' 'Irish' and 'Ulster' only are shown. N = 1291 (1968) 1277 (1978).

Source: E. Moxon-Browne, *Nation, Class and Creed in Northern Ireland.* Aldershot: Gower (1983), p. 6.

In addition to this clear evidence that Catholic identify with the national ethos of the inhabitants of the Republic of Ireland, there is also evidence that they have more contact with them. In answer to the question 'Have you ever travelled to the Republic?' 64% of Catholics but only 37% of Protestants replied that they visited on 'many occasions' or 'regularly.'[13]

Next, we consider the second component of alienation: 'support for policies involving another state in policy-making; and, at the same time abstentionism from the political process within the state.' The largest party in the Catholic community is the Social Democratic and Labour Party (SDLP). It was founded in 1970 as the heir to the Nationalist Party that had carried the banner for Catholic opposition to the regime in Northern Ireland ever since its inception. The aim of the SDLP was, and still is, to act as the party of 'constitutional nationalism' playing the role of 'legitimate opposition' to the majority-dominated political system in the Province. Throughout, the party has been hampered by its inbuilt numerical inferiority and this has caused the party leadership (especially under John Hume) to attempt a broadening of the political debate to include (or involve) at one time or another various external actors e.g. the Dublin government, the British government, the EEC, and the United States.

The latest phase in this broadening process was the establishment of the New Ireland Forum in 1982. This was a conference of four political parties (three from the Republic, and the SDLP from Northern Ireland) whose task it was to map out a blueprint for a 'new Ireland' in which Catholic and Protestant, north and south, would peacefully coexist. The Report from the Forum mapped out three possible scenarios for the future of Ireland but each was eventually ruled out by the British government as being impractical at this time.

For our purposes, the importance of the New Ireland Forum was that it represented an attempt by the SDLP to enlist the involvement of political parties in another state; and thus reflected the alienation of the party from the *status quo* in Northern Ireland. The idea that the government of the Republic should be involved in any political settlement in Northern Ireland is one that is very attractive to Catholics (but distasteful to Protestants who see such involvement as the 'meddling' of a 'foreign power' in the internal affairs of the United Kingdom). Successive opinion surveys show how important the involvement of the Republic is for Catholics. In 1978 78% of Catholics agreed that 'in any political settlement in Northern Ireland the Irish government would have to be consulted' (30% of Protestants). Two years later, in response to the suggestion that the Republic's government 'should be involved in discussions about the future form of government in Northern Ireland' 58% of Catholics (14% of Protestants) agreed.[14] In 1984, when asked if the government of the Republic of Ireland should 'have any say in constitutional changes affecting Northern Ireland, or not' 61% of Catholics said Yes (10% of Protestants).[15]

The two principal political parties, in the Catholic community, the SDLP and Provisional Sinn Fein (PSF), have followed an abstentionist policy with regard to some aspects of the political process in Northern Ireland. Both parties now participate in elections at four different levels of representation: local government; the regional assembly (in Belfast); the national parliament (in London); and the European Parliament (in Strasbourg, France). However, a distinction can be made between the two parties' policy regarding taking up seats after an election. PSF takes its seats in the local government elections but not in the regional assembly or the national parliament, whereas the SDLP takes its seats in the local government elections, in the national and European Parliament, but not in the regional Assembly. The objection of PSF to taking its seats in the regional and national forum is that it does not wish to accord them legitimacy, whereas the local government councils are seen as valuable channels of influence to and from grass-roots opinion. The SDLP takes its seats in all cases except the regional Assembly because it regards the Assembly, established in 1982, as being inadequate since it has no 'Irish dimension' (i.e. no link with the Republic of Ireland). This policy of abstentionism, followed in different degrees by the two Catholic parties means that the Catholic community has virtually no representation in the regional Assembly[16] and only one representative in the Westminster Parliament (out of 17 MP's from Northern Ireland). Abstentionism is clearly a popular policy in the Catholic community since both parties have, between them, held on to their share of the vote in the last three elections. Participation in elections is a way of receiving a mandate for abstentionism. Abstentionism is a clear symptom of political alienation.

Our third component of alienation was 'lack of support for, and hostility to, the judicial system, the forces of law and order, and the penal system.' For the Catholic community, the way the law is applied and enforced is a litmus test of the state's declared intention of providing impartial justice for all its citizens. Consequently, any dissatisfaction must be a major contribution to alienation.

The legitimacy of the state is inextricably tied up with the legal measures required to maintain law and order e.g. the Emergency Provisions Act 1978 and the Prevention of Terrorism Act 1984. Both Acts shift the onus of proof on to the accused in some circumstances e.g. possession of firearms or explosives found on premises in the case of the EPA, and in the case of the PTA, an individual can be required to live in a part of the United Kingdom for reasons which are unspecified and against which it is therefore difficult to construct a defence.[17] A range of offences in both Acts are tried in special courts without a jury. The EPA still contains within it a provision for internment without trial although this is currently in abeyance. However, a source of considerable grievance is that suspects are being remanded without trial for periods of one or two years awaiting their cases to come to court. In March 1984 the House of Commons was told that 108 people had spent more than a year in custody awaiting trial.

Another issue that has become a source of grievance and controversy is the use of 'supergrasses' i.e. the convicting of a number of accused persons on the evidence of one person who is himself accused of a serious crime. There are a number of objections that have been raised to the use of 'supergrasses': an individual may settle old scores by implicating a person he dislikes; the police may be tempted to construct false evidence for the supergrass to use in his 'story;' the payment of money and the granting of immunity from prosecution to the supergrass means that a terrorist may escape trial and punishment. In general, the system of supergrasses has tended to discredit the judicial system and is partly to blame for the alienation of the Catholic community from it.

In the last two years the apparent adoption of a 'shoot to kill' policy on the part of the security forces has further alienated the Catholic community. The members of the police and army are almost exclusively Protestant, the victims of the shootings invariably Catholic. During 1983, seventeen people were killed by either the British Army or the Royal Ulster Constabulary (RUC). Thirteen members of the security forces were charged in connection with seven of these killings. In all cases there were long delays in bringing the cases to court; and in all cases the soldiers and police were acquitted. Even moderate Catholic opinion has been alienated by these apparent travesties of justice. In a recent policy document, the SDLP says:

> The fact that these trials were heard in non-jury courts
> with the repeated appearances of the same judges in
> almost every case gave rise to a serious questioning of
> the impartiality of the judiciary and whether it was now
> legal for British soldiers or the RUC to kill civilians with
> impunity. The situation unfortunately remains un-
> changed with no solider or policeman being convicted of
> a killing of a civilian while on duty in the streets of

Northern Ireland. Such a position has, must and continues to lead, to great alienation from the judicial process.[18]

The use of plastic bullets by the security forces, as a riot control
weapon, has been condemned by the European Parliament and avoided in
all parts of the United Kingdom except Northern Ireland. By the beginning
of 1985 fifteen people had been killed by plastic bullets, some of the victims
being children under 15. The use of plastic bullets has been condemned by
the SDLP since they sometimes kill innocent bystanders; they represent an
excessively dangerous weapon in circumstances where 'minimum force' is
the legal maxim governing riot control; and the rules governing their use are
often broken by the security forces.[19] The failure to prosecute, let alone
convict, those who have killed civilians with plastic bullets has 'contributed
and continues to contribute to the alienation of a substantial and increasing
section of the nationalist population from the judicial system as a whole.'[20]

In sum, the panoply of special laws in Northern Ireland gives the RUC
and Army the legal back-up for stopping, searching, detaining, arresting
and questioning individuals (mainly young unemployed Catholics) and this
constant surveillance by the forces of law and order can itself breed resent-
ment, and a sense of alienation which, in turn, only makes the task of these
forces harder in the future. In a society where national identity is divided, it
would be more conducive to gaining the support of 'Irish' Catholics for the
judicial system if flags, crests, emblems and other symbols of 'British' identity were erased from the court buildings. The alienation of many Catholics
from the judicial system is emphasized when they feel that they are receiving
'British' or 'Protestant' justice in the courts.

In Table 2, we set out some opinion survey evidence that indicates the
extent to which Catholics are unsupportive of the law and order being
dispensed in Northern Ireland.

TABLE 2
Belfast Telegraph–Price Waterhouse Survey, January 1985

Question		Catholics %	Protestants %
How fair do you think the	Very fair	4	37
RUC is in the discharge of	Fair	43	59
its duties in Northern Ireland?			
Question			
Do you think that in the main	Very fairly	4	25
the legal system in Northern	Fairly	32	64
Ireland dispenses justice	Unfairly	37	7
very fairly, fairly, unfairly,	Very unfairly	20	2
or very unfairly?			
Question			
Do you approve or disapprove	Approve	9	86
of the use of plastic bullets	Disapprove	87	8
by the security forces as a			
weapon during riots?			
Question			
Do you think that the evidence	Should be	10	35
of supergrasses should be or	Should not be	81	46
should not be admissible			
without corroboration in the			
trials of those charged with			
terrorist-type offences in			
Northern Ireland?			

Belfast Telegraph-Price Waterhouse Survey   N = 955
January 1985

Source: Belfast Telegraph 6 February 1985, p. 7

The fourth and final component of alienation consists of 'support for political parties that condone violence as a means of effecting political change; support for paramilitary groups; support for violence to overthrow the state.' This component reflects alienation at its most intense: a desire to reject the system by force rather than reform it from within. This dichotomy within the Catholic community - evolution versus revolution - is matched, respectively, by the struggle between SDLP and PSF. These two parties have been competing for the soul of the Catholic community. In the last three elections, for the regional Assembly in 1982, for the Westminster Parliament in 1983, and for the European Parliament in 1984, PSF won 35%, 43% and 38% respectively of the Catholic vote.

The policies of the PSF party, and the extent of the support for the party, embody the more extreme forms of alienation found in the Catholic community. The party sees itself, and is widely perceived to be, the 'political wing' of the IRA. Its principal goal is to expel British influence from Ireland and unite the country. In the meantime, it takes part in all elections, but only takes its seats in the local government councils. It condones the violence of the IRA on the grounds that this violence is a justified response to the presence of British troops on Irish soil.

The rapid emergence of the PSF as an electoral force dates back to the hunger strikes of 1981. These hunger strikes, staged by IRA prisoners claiming recognition of their 'political status,' resulted in ten deaths. The British government resolutely refused to make any concessions, and this obduracy led to the politicisation of a dormant republican (i.e. extreme nationalist) vote in the Catholic community. The demonstrations of popular support for the hunger strikers led to a new awareness of the political leverage that might be derived from participating in elections. These voters had previously stayed at home: now this dormant alienation was transformed into votes for an anti-system party, a party that not only fought elections but also condoned violence as a means of political change. As the party conference heard that November (1981) it was the 'ballot paper in this hand and an Armalite in this hand.' Although the popular support for the hunger strikers never really engulfed the entire Catholic community, the response (or lack of response) from the British Government to the strike went a long way to crystallize hitherto ill-defined alienation on the part of even moderate Catholics who had become frustrated at the lack of political progress within Northern Ireland. Thus the hunger strikes acted as a catalyst: PSF was able to take the tide of opportunity at its flood, and even the SDLP was forced to adopt a more militant posture. Long simmering frustration, and a feeling that even the non-violent constitutionalism of the SDLP was failing to get a response from the British government, served to benefit PSF whose ambivalent attitude towards violence, and more forthright condemnations of Britain, seemed appropriate responses to those who had nothing to lose, and possibly something to gain, by rejecting the *status quo*.

The attitude of the PSF towards violence is undoubtedly part of its electoral appeal. It is also one of the principal features that distinguishes it from SDLP supporters. It is sometimes alleged that a vote for PSF is a 'vote for violence' but this is not wholly true as the figures in Table 3 demonstrate. There is a widespread view within PSF that violence is sometimes justifiable if only because of the lack of any alternative paths towards political change. However, there are other facets of the PSF 'image' that attract voters' support. There are shown in the subsequent table (Table 4).

TABLE 3
MORI Poll, June 1984

Question: How strongly do you agree or disagree that the use of violence can sometimes be justified to bring about political change?

	Sinn Fein %	SDLP %
Agree	70	7
Neither	7	8
Disagree	22	81
D.K./No opinion	1	4

Source: MORI Poll (unpublished) June 1984   N = 1639

TABLE 4
Statements Which Fit Respondents' Ideas of Sinn Fein

	Sinn Fein Voters %		Sinn Fein Voters %
'Extreme'	10	'Has good leaders'	41
'Makes the British take notice of the nationalists'	84	'I've always supported the party's views'	42
'Tough'	34	'Out of touch'	2
'Active in the local community'	56	'Behind the times'	2
'Evil'	2	'Trustworthy'	21
'Has good policies'	58	'Caring'	16
'Offers most hope of a solution to the troubles'	51	'Moderate'	9
		'Too cooperative with Britain'	1
'Represents people like me'	58		

Source: MORI Poll (unpublished) June 1984   N = 562

We have already established that there is considerable support among PSF voters for the use of violence to bring about political change. We have also seen (in Table 4) that the appeal of the party is broader than a mere mandate for the gunman. Clearly, PSF voters perceive their party as being well-led, active in local communities, representative of its grass-roots and, above all, (cited by 84% of PSF voters) able to make the British government take notice of nationalist demands. As the PSF is the 'political wing' of the IRA it is worth considering the views taken by PSF supporters towards the IRA. Does the link between the party and the paramilitary organization constitute a life-support system for the party? The answer appears to be 'yes.' Whereas 39% of SDLP voters agree that the 'IRA are basically patriots and idealists,' this figure rises to 77% for PSF voters.[21] On the more specific policy question of whether PSF should 'renounce the armed campaign of the IRA' only 22% of PSF voters agree (exactly the same percentage that is against violence for political change in Table 3).

The support for the violence of the IRA among four out of five of PSF voters represents the extreme point on the continuum of 'alienation' ranging across our four 'components:' at one extreme, a desire to work within the system, but at the other a marked inclination to overthrow the system by force. An investigation of the principal demographic features of the PSF support shows it to be young, from the lower socioeconomic strata, often unemployed, and more likely to be male than female. Some of these features of PSF support can be seen in Table 5, while comparisons with the SDLP can be made.

TABLE 5
The PSF and the SDLP

	Age	PSF	SDLP
	18-34	38%	46%
	35-54	22%	58%
	55+	16%	65%
	Gender	**PSF**	**SDLP**
	Male	34%	54%
	Female	24%	64%
	Socioeconomic status	**PSF**	**SDLP**
A B C 1	20%	66%	
	C2DE	33%	57%

Source: MORI Poll (unpublished) June 1984   *N = 457*

Comparisons with the 'constitutional' SDLP are instructive, PSF is a young party and is firmly based in the lower socioeconomic echelons of the Catholic community. About 50% of PSF voters are under 34 (compared with 29% of SDLP voters). One-fifth of PSF support comes from non-manual socioeconomic groups, while one-third of SDLP support does. 31% of PSF supporters are unemployed; but only 13% of SDLP supporters. Asked what the cause of the Northern Ireland problem is, PSF supporters are more likely to see it as a clash of national identity, and less likely to see it as a problem of 'terrorism' than SDLP supporters. Both Catholic parties evince strong dissatisfaction with the British Government's handling of the situation in the Province, but this dissatisfaction is much stronger in PSF than it is in the SDLP. The crucial difference between the two parties is their attitudes towards violence. As we have seen (see Table 3) PSF supporters are much more likely to condone violence than SDLP supporters and while 29% of PSF voters say they 'strongly' agree that violence is sometimes justified, only 1% of SDLP voters fall into this extreme category.[22]

Conclusion: policy implications

Faced with widespread alienation within the Catholic community, ranging from those who accept the status quo and are willing to make it work, through to those who see violent change as the only hope of reform, the British government is forced to steer a middle course between the men of violence and the 'constitutional' politicians. But, unfortunately, concessions made to the latter are often seen, and claimed, as concessions to the former.

Since 1969, when the present spate of civil unrest erupted, the British government has responded to the crisis along three avenues: security, economics, politics. In the political field, there have been several attempts to construct a framework of devolved government within which the two communities could cooperate to their mutual benefit. So far, this has not been achieved. The brief power-sharing experiment of 1974 lasted five months but was eventually wrecked by Loyalist (i.e. extreme Protestant) reactions to the proposed North-South Council of Ireland which was perceived as the thin end of a wedge that would lead to a united Ireland. The present 78-man Assembly in Belfast is the latest experiment. Its role is purely advisory and consultative although the intention is that legislative powers could be devolved to it if there was sufficient cross-community consensus to warrant it. At the moment this seems unlikely as the two Catholic parties, PSF and the SDLP, are boycotting the Assembly because it excludes both an 'Irish dimension' (i.e. with the Republic) and any real recognition of Irish identity among Catholics in Northern Ireland. Since 1973, proportional representation has been introduced into local and regional elections in Northern Ireland (a novelty in the United Kingdom) with the aim of enhancing the influence of the Catholic minority in political affairs. While this has undoubtedly happened, it has also led to the splitting of the confessional 'blocs,' into two parties each, so that extremists on both sides now have parties to themselves (PSF for the Catholics, DUP for the Protestants). The prospects for reconciliation between moderates in each community is now more remote because the 'moderate' parties (OUP for Protestants, SDLP for Catholics) have to look over their shoulders at the more militant policies of the parties on their flanks.

Security policy has made progress in its primary aim: the reduction in the number of fatalities in the Province. In 1972 over four hundred people died in the region; now the annual total is less than one hundred. The cost has been high in terms of alienating the Catholic community. Special legislation giving the police wide powers of arrest, detention, and interrogation; long periods of remand; the abolition of juries for many trials; the use of supergrasses; the apparent immunity from conviction of policemen or soldiers who murder civilians; and the overwhelming Protestant composition of the security forces: all these facets of the security policy of the Government combine to minimize the legitimacy of the state in the eyes of the Catholic community. The policy of 'Ulsterisation' - the policy of transferring the burden of security to locally recruited personnel - has done little to kindle hope in the Catholic community that law and order will be impartially administered.

Economic policy has consisted of building up the infrastructure of the Province - roads, houses, harbours, energy supplies - so that foreign investment will stimulate greater employment opportunities. Per capita expenditure is higher in the Province than in the rest of the United Kingdom: and so is the dependence on welfare handouts.

The Government's policy towards PSF consists of a 'twin-track' approach: encouraging constitutional nationalism (as expressed in the SDLP) and ostracising PSF representatives at Ministerial level. However, PSF is a legal party and both civil servants and local councillors are expected to deal with them in the normal way. This partial boycott of PSF representatives is defended on the grounds that PSF refuses to condemn violence, and as a way of bolstering the 'parliamentary' tactics of the SDLP.

Faced by an alienated minority, a central government has, in theory, a range of options extending from total suppression of the minority to a full recognition of its separate identity *via* the creation of a separate state. Neither of these extreme policies is relevant to Northern Ireland since suppression of a minority consisting of 40% of the population is unthinkable, and territorial separateness is ruled out by the intermingling of the two communities. In between these extremes there lies a variety of options including consociationalism, cantonisation, total absorption, pluralism and relocation. So far, the Government has been attempting a policy of 'integration' or 'homogenisation' - a policy of treating the Catholic community as equal citizens of the United Kingdom: and much progress has been made in legislating away discriminatory practices and providing adequate economic resources. But it looks as if even this policy, even if successful, will have to make way for a new policy of pluralism (or more strictly 'binationalism') in order to satisfy the aspirations of the militant elements in the Catholic community. Already there have been straws in the wind: talk of the 'Irish identity' in Government circles, the financing of an Irish speaking school in Belfast, the refusal to proscribe PSF, and most recently the banning of provocative Protestant marches through Catholic residential areas. Otherwise, very little has been done officially to grant the Irish identity of Catholics its legitimate place in Northern Ireland, or to give Catholics access to policy-making in a meaningful sense, or to ensure that law, order and justice apply to all without fear or favour. If alienation means 'feeling a stranger in one's own country' then there is scope for making the Catholic community feel that they have a stake in the society they inhabit: if one is treated like an outsider, it is likely that one will behave like an outsider.

Attempts by the Government to promote 'binationalism' run into the problem of Protestant opposition. Lately, one has heard the phrase 'Protestant alienation' - a term loosely referring to the reactions of IRA violence, and 'reforms' by the Government to enhance Catholic political and economic participation. The situation is not a bi-polar one with the Protestants and British ranged against the Catholic community. On the contrary the situation is triangular: both communities are to some extent alienated from British rule,[23] albeit for different reasons and to different degrees. Thus the strategy of the Government, or any government faced by a multi-ethnic society, has to be that of 'balancing' interests and seeking the issues that bind rather than those that divide. Given the demographic trends in Northern Ireland, it seems advisable for the 'majority' of today to negotiate the terms for survival of tomorrow's minority.

Notes

[1]*The Shorter Oxford English Dictionary,* Oxford: Clarendon (1973).

[2]Published in the summer of 1984.

[3]Bishop Cahal Daly, *Communities Without Consensus.* Dublin: Irish Messenger Publications (1984), p. 5.

[4]See D. Eversley and V. Herr, *The Roman Catholic Population of Northern Ireland in 1981: A Revised Estimate.* Belfast: Fair Employment Agency (1985), p. 1.

[5]*Ibid.*

[6]D. Watt (ed), *The Constitution of Northern Ireland: Problems and Prospects.* London: Heinemann (1981), p. 88.

[7]See E. Moxon-Browne, *Nation, Class and Creed in Northern Ireland.* Aldershot: Gower (1983), p. 84.

[8]See A. Lijphart, 'Review Article: The Northern Ireland Problem: Case Theories and Solutions' in *British Journal of Political Science,* vol. 5.

[9]Fair Employment Agency, *Report of an Investigation by the FEA for Northern Ireland into the non-industrial Civil Service.* Belfast: FEA (1983), p. 65.

[10]R.J. Cormack and R.D. Osborne (eds), *Religion, Education and Employment: Aspects of Equal Opportunity in Northern Ireland.* Belfast: Appletree Press (1983), pp. 25-41.

[11]E. Moxon-Browne, *op.cit.,* p. 83.

[12]R. Rose, *Government Without Consensus.* London: Faber (1971), p. 209.

[13]E. Moxon-Browne, *op.cit.,* p. 30.

[14]*Ibid.,* p. 20.

[15]LWT/MORI Poll (May 1984) N = 1028 (Quota sample).

[16]There are, however, five Catholics in the transectarian Alliance Party which has ten seats in the Assembly.

[17]C. Scorer and P. Hewitt, *The Prevention of Terrorism Act.* London: NCCL (1981).

[18]SDLP, *'Justice' in Northern Ireland.* Belfast: SDLP (January 1983) mimeo pp. 11-12.

[19]*Ibid.*

[20]*Ibid.*

[21]MORI Poll (unpublished) June 1984.

[22]*Ibid.*

[23]See E. Moxon-Browne, *op.cit.,* p. 56.

Fighting Terrorism in Democratic Societies

11

WILLIAM LASSER

Can a free society fight terrorism effectively at home and abroad without compromising the values and principles that make it free? Is it possible to fight terrorism at home and abroad without sacrificing our commitment to liberty, democracy, individual rights, due process of law, and limited government? As the terrorist threat escalates, the United States and its Western allies will find increasing urgency in Abraham Lincoln's disturbing question: "Must a government, of necessity, be too strong for the liberties of its own people, or too weak to maintain its own existence?"[1]

No one questions the necessity of combatting terrorism; the impact of even a few terrorist incidents on the quality of life in any society can be devastating. Governmental attempts to deal with terrorism, however, may also present a serious threat to a free society, by threatening the civil rights and civil liberties of the individuals who make up that society. The effort to combat terrorism may be detrimental to civil rights and civil liberties in three ways: first, governments facing a specific terrorist threat may seek to short-circuit normal legal and judicial processes, thus depriving terrorists or suspected terrorists of their rights under law; second, governments under severe pressure may find it necessary to restrict the civil rights and civil liberties not only of specific suspects but of a whole group of citizens, or even of the entire population; finally, and perhaps most insidiously, persistent and escalating terrorism may in the long run weaken the Western democracies' dedication to preserving freedom and due process of law, transforming the very nature of Western society in the process.

In trying to understand the implications of fighting terrorism in free societies, it is necessary to piece together evidence from a variety of scattered sources. Fortunately for U.S. citizens, the United States does not have extensive experience in dealing with terrorist organizations, and thus there is a limited body of both case law and of empirical evidence on the subject. Unfortunately, the experience of other Western democracies, especially the United Kingdom, is more extensive, and there is much to be learned from the British experience. This chapter attempts to describe the civil liberties implications of a wide variety of terrorist threats, and in the end focuses on three of the most severe historical examples: Lincoln's attempts to deal with the secessionist threat in 1861; the internment of Japanese-Americans on the West Coast during World War II; and the British experience in Northern Ireland. The approach here is exploratory and tentative; the goal is simply to raise the important questions and to sharpen the ongoing debate.

Categories of Terrorist Activity

Even a cursory glance at the scholarly literature on terrorism makes it clear that the term embraces a wide variety of diverse phenomena. Although scholars have not agreed on a definition, "terrorism" is most generally used to denote "the use of violence, in a nonmilitary context, to achieve political goals."[2] Although this traditional definition is unobjectionable, it will be more helpful in seeking to understand the implications of terrorism for civil rights and civil liberties to begin with a brief typology of terrorism, organized according to the relative seriousness of the threat to civil liberties. This typology is meant to be illustrative rather than exhaustive, and is intended to serve only as a starting point for the discussion.[3] The four categories of terrorist activity to be considered, ranked according to the potential threat to civil liberties caused by government attempts to combat terrorism are: (1) terrorism directed against U.S. nationals—whether civilian, military, or diplomatic—abroad, or against U.S. property abroad, by foreign nationals, whether acting independently or on behalf of a sovereign state; (2) terrorism directed against persons or property within the United States by foreign nationals; (3) terrorism directed against persons or property within the United States by splinter groups of U.S. citizens; and (4) terrorism directed against persons or property within the United States as part of a massive rebellion or incipient civil war.

Terrorism Directed Against U.S. Nationals
Abroad or Against U.S. Property Abroad

This category of terrorist activities comprises most of the attacks directed at the United States to date, and is what U.S. citizens commonly think of when they think of terrorism. Incidents falling into this category include the massacre of the U.S. marines in Beirut in 1983; the taking of the U.S. embassy in Teheran in 1979; the hijacking of T.W.A. flight #847 in 1985; and countless others. This category is also the least problematical from the point of view of civil liberties. While important civil liberties questions do arise in such cases, two critical factors minimize the problem: the incidents take place on foreign soil, as do the investigation of the incident and the apprehension, if possible, of the suspects; and the suspects, at least until brought into U.S. custody, do not enjoy the full panoply of rights held by persons within the jurisdiction of the United States. Thus, for example, a suspect can be forcibly abducted from a foreign country and brought within the jurisdiction of the United States for trial,[4] and may not be fully protected by the Fourth Amendment against unreasonable searches and seizures.[5] While the United States might be bound by moral obligations, international law, or political realities in dealing with terrorism suspects, these requirements do not pose civil liberties problems *per se*.

Indeed, one way to deal with terrorism suspects is to regard them as "enemies" of the United States and thus subject to the laws of war rather than the laws of civil society. "Terrorism is war without limits," writes Neil C. Livingston, "and unless the state can respond accordingly, measure for measure, it will be at a considerable disadvantage when confronted with an enemy that is not restrained by the same rules that it is."[6] Enemy combatants in wartime are at risk of attack or capture merely because of their identification with and membership in the enemy army; it is not necessary under international law to demonstrate that specific individuals were themselves engaged in specific enemy operations. Enemy prisoners of war are entitled to the protections of international law, including the Geneva Conventions, including the right to withhold information from their captors, to communicate with relatives, and to have access to neutral parties.[7] Obviously, however, they are not accorded due process of law and can be interned, indefinitely, until the cessation of hostilities.

Declaring terrorists to be "enemies" in the classic sense has obvious advantages. Above all, it would eliminate the moral or legal necessity of proving individual guilt before actions can be taken against particular suspects. The Western democracies, however, have been reluctant to accord terrorists the status of formal "enemies," and have instead chosen to regard them, in effect, as pirates—that is, as international criminals whose acts violate not only the law of a particular nation but international law as well. Various terrorist acts are defined as crimes both in numerous international agreements and in domestic laws of many countries.[8] Individuals committing terrorist acts, whether acting on their own or on behalf of a sovereign nation, can be seized and arrested by any nation (including the United States) and can be tried as criminals. Classifying terrorists as criminals rather than as enemies serves a dual purpose: it denies to the individuals the more noble status that would come from regarding them as "soldiers"; and it denies to the terrorists' cause the more noble status that would come from regarding it as analogous to the legitimate interests of sovereign states. It does mean, however, that terrorists are entitled to a trial if and when they are brought into the United States or any other democratic country; and that evidence linking a specific suspect to a specific incident must be obtained and the link proved beyond a reasonable doubt. In fact, attempts by the United States to seize and try suspected terrorists have been largely unsuccessful.

Because U.S. nationals are involved only as victims in category 1 cases, and because the acts occur outside the United States, the civil liberties concerns growing out of such incidents are relatively minor and tangential. Serious issues were raised in 1984, however, when the United States enacted legislation designed to strengthen the government's hand in fighting international terrorism.

What bothered civil libertarians most in the 1984 proposals was a bill, S. 2626, that would have made it "unlawful for any national of the United States . . . [to] serve in, or act in concert with . . . [or] provide any logistical, mechanical, maintenance or similar support" to groups or countries designated as terrorists by the secretary of state.[9] The broad language of the proposed legislation, according to civil libertarians, would have given the secretary of state sole discretion to outlaw support for certain countries, factions, or groups and then make it a crime for U.S. citizens to support that country or group, even though their support may be directed to legitimate political or humanitarian goals. The proposed legislation, the American Civil Liberties Union argued, would have criminalized activities clearly protected by the First Amendment and not intended to aid or abet terrorist acts of force or violence.[10] For example, the ACLU contended, the bill would have made it illegal for an American to write pamphlets on behalf of an outlawed organization; to speak out on behalf of such a group; to act as an attorney for a member of such a group on a paid or volunteer basis; or to send money to aid the lawful, nonviolent activities of such a group.[11] In the end, neither the House nor the Senate Judiciary Committees allowed the legislation to see the light of day.

The ACLU's concerns about S. 2626 raise valid and important civil liberties concerns, but the major lesson of the 1984 debate is that legislation to counter international terrorism must be drafted with extreme caution. The goals of S. 2626 could have been achieved, as the ACLU pointed out, by passage of legislation outlawing the aiding and abetting of specific terrorist acts, thus eliminating the conclusive determination of terrorist status by the secretary of state and limiting the scope of the legislation to clearly criminal activities.

Terrorism Within the United States by Foreign Nationals

When the focus of terrorist activities shifts from the foreign to the domestic arena, the potential threat to civil liberties increases dramatically. This increased threat arises precisely because of the necessity of increased security measures, including greater police surveillance and intelligence-gathering activity. Certainly, as Paul Wilkinson points out, "Sane and fair-minded people look eagerly and gratefully to growing evidence of police effectiveness in securing the capture and conviction of terrorist murderers, for it is ordinary people—men, women, and children, who have suffered death, injury, and terror in successive terrorist attacks."[12] Increased police activity, however, even though desirable and necessary, does carry with it a corresponding threat to individual rights.

As long as the terrorists themselves are foreign nationals, however, the threat to civil liberties is minimized. Under such circumstances the initial line of defense against terror is border security. Interdiction of the flow of arms and careful scrutiny of persons seeking to enter the United States can of course be effective preventatives without excessively endangering liberty. Here the primary danger is the exclusion of aliens seeking to enter the United States simply because of their association with a group or regime suspected of or known to participate in terrorist activity. Such individuals, while not strictly speaking possessing the legal right to enter the United States, may nonetheless contribute significantly to public debate within this country, and their exclusion may deprive U.S. citizens of the freedom to hear their point of view, support their legitimate political activities, or influence U.S. government policy. Such exclusions, moreover, are typically carried out unilaterally by the executive branch, and may be influenced by ideological as well as security considerations.

Dealing with potential or suspected foreign terrorists already within the United States becomes, in effect, a problem in intelligence-gathering and effective surveillance. While such measures pose little threat to the general population, the focus on suspected terrorists of a particular ethnic, racial, religious, or national group could pose serious problems of equal protection, if individuals (whether citizens or resident aliens) are singled out for disparate treatment solely on invidious grounds. This problem, clearly revealed by the Japanese internment cases, is treated more fully in the next section.

*Terrorism Within the United States by
Splinter Groups of U.S. Citizens*

When individual citizens or groups of citizens engage in terrorist activity, the terrorist threat becomes dramatically more difficult to deal with and the potential threat to civil liberties from police action against the terrorists becomes correspondingly greater. The United States has had limited experience with such groups. Between 1973 and 1982, for example, less than 1 percent of worldwide terrorist incidents occurred in the United States, and only part of these were the work of domestic terrorists.[13] In the 1960s there was some violence on the part of some radical groups, such as the Weathermen; more recently there have been threats of terrorism from Puerto Rican extremists. In the mid-1980s the most serious terrorist threats of this type come from neo-Nazis and other white supremacists trained in paramilitary operations.[14]

One serious danger to civil liberties arising out of the attempt to combat internal terrorism is the risk of governmental interference in or harassment of legitimate political activity. This problem is particularly acute when the suspected terrorists are U.S. citizens. Frequently, a single organization may comprise a few individuals engaged in potentially illegal activity and a much larger number involved in activity protected under the First Amendment; or the same individuals may be involved in licit and illicit activities at different times and in different places.

In a large number of cases, the Supreme Court has recognized both the legitimacy of police surveillance and the potential threat to civil liberties created by such surveillance. In *United States* v. *U.S. District Court,* for example, Justice Powell wrote that

> We recognize that domestic security surveillances may involve different policy and practical considerations from the surveillance of "ordinary crime." The gathering of security intelligence is often long range and involves the interrelation of various sources and types of information. The exact targets of surveillance may be more difficult to identify. . . . Often, too, the emphasis of domestic intelligence gathering is on the prevention of unlawful activity or the enhancement of the Government's preparedness for some possible future crisis or emergency. Thus the focus of domestic surveillance may be less precise than that directed against more conventional types of crime.[15]

In the same opinion, however, Justice Powell warned that national security surveillance cases also require special care because of the First Amendment concerns involved. He concluded:

> The price of lawful dissent must not be a dread of subjection to an unchecked surveillance power. Nor must the fear of unauthorized official eavesdropping deter vigorous citizen dissent and discussion of Government action in private conversation. For private dissent, no less than open public discourse, is essential to our free society.[16]

Because governmental surveillance raises both First and Fourth Amendment (search and seizure) concerns, the Supreme Court has recognized that governmental surveillance must not sweep so broadly as to "chill" legitimate political activity. Moreover, the Court has rejected the claim that the president has the inherent power to engage in wiretapping and other surveillance activity, even when based on national security concerns.[17]

Another serious threat to civil liberties arises when the government stigmatizes an entire racial, ethnic, or national group on the basis of allegedly illegal activity by some small fraction of that group. Especially at times of national crisis,

115

racial or ethnic prejudice can run high, and there may be a tendency, justified perhaps on the grounds of efficiency, to treat all members of a certain group as suspects.

One need look no further than the World War II Japanese internment cases for an example of the danger. Faced with the possibility of invasion and unwilling or unable to separate loyal U.S. citizens from saboteurs, the U.S. Army excluded "all persons of Japanese ancestry" from designated areas on the West Coast of the United States. Those who could make arrangements to live elsewhere were required to leave the West Coast; the rest were interned in detention camps. The U.S. Supreme Court, while recognizing that distinctions based on race must be subjected to "the most rigid scrutiny," upheld the exclusion and detention in *Korematsu* v. *United States*: the security measures were necessarily applied to all Japanese-Americans, the Court held, "because of the presence of an unascertained number of disloyal members of that group, most of whom we have no doubt were loyal to this country." The majority opinion stressed the need to defer to the judgment of Congress and the appropriate military authorities and denied that "racial prejudice" was an issue. "Nothing short of apprehension by the proper military authorities of the gravest imminent danger to the public safety can constitutionally justify" such action, wrote Justice Black. But, the Court concluded, the current case was one of those extraordinary circumstances.[18]

Justice Murphy's vehement dissent in *Korematsu,* which has grown in stature over the decades, scored the military for making its decisions not out of legitimate security concerns but on the basis of "misinformation, half-truths and insinuations that for years have been directed against Japanese-Americans by people with racial and economic prejudices."[19] Although *Korematsu* has been thoroughly discredited, examples of guilt-by-association on racial or ethnic grounds still occur, particularly when terrorism causes emotions and tempers to run high. One need only note the displays of anti-Iranian sentiment in the United States in 1979–1980, or scattered comments regarding the potential terrorist threat from the Mexican-American and U.S. Muslim communities.[20]

Terrorism Against Persons or Property Within the
United States as Part of a Massive Rebellion
or "Incipient Civil War."[21]

When the battle against domestic terrorism ceases to be a fight against a small number of criminals and becomes, or threatens to become, a civil war, the government's approach to the crisis, and the corresponding threat to civil liberties, changes dramatically. "When troops are really needed in a liberal state to restore and maintain law and order," writes Paul Wilkinson, "by definition the conditions of normal policing do not obtain. The very fabric of the state and the life, safety and property of its citizens are under armed attack by ruthless and fanatical opponents." Under such circumstances, Wilkinson concludes, "There is only one sensible objective for an army engaged in internal war, and this is to root out and defeat the enemy, to destroy the insurgent movement as a military and political force so that the constitution and laws can be restored and upheld."[22] As Wilkinson's language suggests, the outlook for civil liberties in such circumstances—such as the U.S. Civil War or the British struggle to maintain order in Northern Ireland—is clear, and not encouraging. In times of war, the laws are silent.

Governments faced with a massive revolutionary threat choose from a common set of measures designed to weaken and ultimately strangle the enemy. These include strict controls on acquiring and possessing firearms; adoption of legislation making membership in or support for the revolutionary organization a crime; establishment of a "civil registration" program including mandatory identity cards for all citizens and resident aliens; suspension of the writ of *habeas corpus,* thus permitting the arrest and detention of suspects without charge; expansion of search and seizure powers; replacement of civilian justice systems with military or administrative tribunals; adoption of stiff penalties for convicted rebels, including widespread use of the death sentence; curtailment of free speech and assembly rights; censorship or suppression of the news media; and suspension of democratic political processes for the duration of the conflict.[23]

In 1861, for example, Abraham Lincoln dealt with the secessionist threat by assuming virtually complete control of the U.S. government between the attack on Fort Sumter in April and the reconvening of the U.S. Congress in July. During that period, besides calling out the militia and ordering a blockade of southern ports, Lincoln authorized the army to suspend the writ of *habeas corpus* "at any point or in the vicinity of any military line which is now or which shall be used between the city of Philadelphia and the city of Washington." Lincoln also closed the mails to "treasonable correspondence" and authorized the civil or military arrest of any persons engaged in or about to be engaged in "disloyal and treasonable practices."[24] Later in the war Lincoln authorized an even broader suspension of civil rights and civil liberties, including allowing the military trial of civilians and the suspension of the writ of *habeas corpus* across the United States. Though eventually the Supreme Court held some of these practices unconstitutional—in particular the military trial of civilians in areas where the civilian courts were still open—the Court was hardly bold in its defense of civil liberties while the war was still on.[25]

The British experience in Northern Ireland is no more encouraging for civil libertarians. In 1973, faced with a growing security problem in Northern Ireland, the British Parliament responded with legislation outlawing the IRA and banning public displays of support for the organization; permitting the arrest and detention of suspected terrorists without charge; expanding security checks on travelers entering or leaving Britain; reversing the burden of proof in certain criminal cases, thus requiring the suspect to prove innocence instead of requiring the government to prove guilt; and permitting the detention, deportation, and exclusion of suspected terrorists without conviction of a crime in a court of law.[26] In fact, however, the damage to civil liberties exceeded even these statutory measures. According to one study,

> . . . there is evidence that the procedure for arrest and questioning and for extra-judicial detention has been abused. The security officers have in some areas mounted a "dredging" operation based on widespread screening. This has resulted, in our view, in large numbers of wholly innocent persons being arrested and large numbers whose involvement in terrorist activities is relatively unimportant being detained.[27]

The use of the emergency provisions to suppress legitimate political activity has also been noted; for example,

117

> although the selling of Republican newspapers is not an of-
> fence [sic], the vendors could be arrested and held under Part
> I [of the Temporary Provisions Act]. Clearly, from the police
> standpoint, disseminating information of a Republican na-
> ture, albeit not in support of terrorism, is itself grounds for
> reasonable suspicion of support[ing], assisting, or contribut-
> ing to a proscribed organisation [sic].[28]

And, although in theory the Temporary Provisions Act was to be temporary, in fact it was reauthorized year after year; the danger, as the National Council for Civil Liberties (NCLC) put it at the time, is that "the new procedures will come to be accepted as the norm" in Northern Ireland, and even, perhaps, elsewhere in Great Britain.[29]

The U.S. Civil War and the Northern Ireland experiences make it quite clear that even those societies most dedicated to the rule of law and the protection of individual liberty are prone to extreme measures when faced with a sizable terrorist threat at home. The United States, even with its written Constitution enforced by the Supreme Court's power of judicial review, does not seem to be exempt from this tendency.

Strategies to Combat Terrorism

Even this brief overview of the potential conflict between fighting terrorism and preserving civil liberties makes several lessons clear. First, and most impor-tant, a concern for civil liberties must be a major part of any antiterrorist strategy adopted by a democratic society. The maintenance of democratic processes and the rule of law, writes Wilkinson,

> overrides in importance even the objective of eliminating ter-
> rorism and political violence as such. Any bloody tyrant can
> "solve" the problem of political violence if he is prepared to
> sacrifice all considerations of humanity, and to trample down
> all constitutional and judicial rights.[30]

Those who devise and carry out antiterrorist policies must not forget that their aim is not simply to eradicate the terrorist threat, but to do so while at the same time preserving civil rights and civil liberties to the greatest extent possible.

Dedication to the maintenance of civil rights and civil liberties means more than merely paying lip service to the Constitution or to the rule of law. Throughout the scholarly literature on terrorism, there is a disturbing tendency among scholars to endorse the principle of preserving civil liberties while simultaneously suggest-ing policies that undermine those liberties. One scholar, for example, while warn-ing against "the easy move to repression as a counter to terrorism," nonetheless recommends limiting rights of assembly, requiring identification cards, allowing internment without trial, and limiting the ability of the media to report terrorist acts, as "parts of an anti-terrorist campaign."[31] Another, cautioning against both "overreacting and underreacting to terrorism," advocates "strict passport and iden-tity control, including the issuance of national identity cards" and adds, "Citizens innocent of crimes should have little to fear from such methods; they will be only slightly inconvenienced."[32]

Second, as the above typology makes clear, the response to terrorism must be strictly limited to what is absolutely necessary to protect the lives and property of government officials and civilians. Certainly there is room for a margin of safety, but the costs of erring on the side of restricting freedom are too great to be taken lightly. The nature of each potential terrorist threat must be carefully identified, and the responses made commensurate with the threat. Governments cannot afford to have but one antiterrorist strategy; they need several, each tailored as precisely as possible to the potential threat and each designed to minimize damage to individual rights. A strategy that would be necessary to combat a large-scale domestic security threat would be inappropriate if the terrorists represented only isolated splinter groups. Too often conferences are held and papers presented on such topics as "Terrorism: What Should Be Our Response?" when a more helpful and ultimately safer approach would be "Terrorism: What Should Be Our *Responses?*"[33]

Third, antiterrorist strategies should be flexible, allowing for both escalation and deescalation of the antiterrorist response as the situation warrants. Antiterrorism experts will have no difficulty designing a strategy that can increase in scope or intensity to meet worsening circumstances; the record suggests that it is more difficult to design a strategy that will do the opposite. As the Northern Ireland case demonstrates, it is not enough for legislation to expire automatically every six or twelve months, for legislative and executive inertia and public anxiety make renewal of the emergency legislation almost automatic. Instead, emergency legislation must set out specific conditions that must be met on a continuing basis in order for particular measures to remain in effect; if those conditions are not met, then certain provisions—but not necessarily the entire package—would automatically expire.

Designing legislation that meets these three conditions is difficult at any time, but it is next to impossible once the terrorist threat is imminent. Under conditions of impending disaster, policymakers will be forced to make hurried and poorly thought-out decisions and will be inclined to overestimate the terrorist threat and underestimate the consequent damage to civil liberties. The rhetoric of public officials and heightened media coverage will do little to create the kind of atmosphere necessary for reasonable and responsible emergency policies. The first Temporary Provisions Act, for example, passed in 1974 only eight days after brutal terrorist attacks in two Birmingham pubs killed twenty and injured 180 people. The bill was debated for only twelve hours in the House of Commons and was approved the following morning by the House of Lords.[34] In this respect the Reagan administration proposals in 1984 served an important purpose, generating two sets of hearings on Capitol Hill and providing the impetus for an important debate well in advance of any crisis.

Finally, public officials and other public opinion leaders must be careful not to engage in inflammatory rhetoric that serves to overstate the terrorist threat and erode concern over civil liberties. History shows how easy it is to convince even a democratic society that civil rights and civil liberties must yield to an internal or external security threat. Irresponsible rhetoric only makes the loss of civil liberties

119

more likely in the long run, without meaningfully increasing our protection against terrorism. Instead, those responsible for developing and carrying out antiterrorist policies must take the time to understand the legitimate concerns of civil libertarians, communicate those concerns to the general public, and incorporate them into their rhetoric and policy.

Notes

1. Roy P. Basler, *The Collected Works of Abraham Lincoln,* vol. 4 (New Brunswick, N.J.: Rutgers University Press, 1953), p. 426.

2. Steven Anzovin, *Terrorism* (New York: H. W. Wilson Co., 1986), p. 7.

3. For clarity, I present much of the following from the standpoint of the United States, although the typology could be applied to terrorist threats or actions against any of the Western democracies.

4. Ker v. Illinois, 119 U.S. 437 (1886); Frisbie v. Collins, 342 U.S. 519 (1952).

5. See United States v. Best, 184 F. 2d 131 (C.A. 1st Cir.).

6. Neil C. Livingston, *The War Against Terrorism* (Lexington, Mass.: Lexington Books, 1978), p. 155.

7. Geneva Convention, 1949.

8. Since 1961, for example, the United States has regarded the hijacking of aircraft (a favorite terrorist activity) as "air piracy," punishable as piracy under international law. See Gerhard von Glahn, *Law Among Nations* (New York: Macmillan, 1986), pp. 297–300, for a summary of international agreements on terrorism.

9. U.S. Congress, Senate, S. 2626, A bill "to prohibit the training, supporting, or inducing of terrorism, and for other purposes." 98th Cong., 2d sess.

10. U.S. Congress, Senate, *Legislative Initiatives to Curb Domestic and International Terrorism. Hearings Before the Subcommittee on Security and Terrorism of the Committee on the Judiciary,* 98th Cong., 2d sess., 1984, pp. 146–147.

11. *Ibid.,* pp. 147–149.

12. Paul Wilkinson, *Terrorism and the Liberal State* (New York: New York University Press, 1986), p. 144.

13. *Legislative Initiatives to Curb Domestic and International Terrorism,* p. 61.

14. Anzovin, *Terrorism,* p. 22.

15. U.S. v. U.S. District Court, 407 U.S. 297 (1972), at 322.

16. *Ibid.,* at 314.

17. *Ibid.*

18. Korematsu v. United States, 323 U.S. 214 (1944), at 216, 218–219, 223, 218.

19. *Ibid.,* at 239.

20. U.S. Congress, House, *Domestic Security Measures Relating to Terrorism. Hearings Before the Subcommittee on Civil and Constitutional Rights of the Committee on the Judiciary,* 98th Cong., 2d sess., 1984, p. 133.

21. Wilkinson, *Terrorism and the Liberal State,* p. 156.

22. *Ibid.,* pp. 157–158.

23. Adopted from Christopher Hewitt, *The Effectiveness of Anti-Terrorist Policies* (Lanham, Md.: University Press of America, 1984), pp. 61–64.

24. Clinton Rossiter, *Constitutional Dictatorship: Crisis Government in the Modern Democracies* (New York: Harcourt, Brace, and World, 1963), pp. 227–228.

25. *Ex Parte* Milligan, 4 Wallace 2 (1866). For the Court's cavalier treatment of civil liberties during the war, see The Prize Cases, 2 Black 635 (1863) and *Ex Parte* Vallandingham, 1 Wallace 243 (1864).

26. Grant Wardlaw, *Political Terrorism: Theory, Tactics, and Counter-Measures* (Cambridge: Cambridge University Press, 1982), p. 127; Merlyn Rees, "Terror in Ireland—and Britain's Response," in Paul Wilkinson, ed., *British Perspectives on Terrorism* (London: Allen & Unwin, 1981), p. 84.

27. Kevin Boyle, Tom Hadden, and Paddy Hillyard, "The Facts on Internment in Northern Ireland," in Ronald D. Crelinsten, Danielle Laberge-Altmejd, and Denis Szabo, *Terrorism and Criminal Justice: An International Perspective* (Lexington, Mass.: Lexington Books, 1978), p. 112.

28. Wardlaw, *Political Terrorism,* p. 129.

29. *Ibid.,* p. 128.

30. Paul Wilkinson, quoted in Wardlaw, *Political Terrorism,* p. 69.

31. Wardlaw, *Political Terrorism,* pp. 66–69.

32. Livingstone, *War Against Terrorism,* pp. 115, 166–167.

33. See, for example, "Terrorism: What Should Be Our Response?" (Washington: American Enterprise Institute, 1982).

34. Wardlaw, *Political Terrorism,* pp. 126–127. The Temporary Provisions Act had been prepared earlier, as Wilkinson notes (Wilkinson, *Terrorism and the Liberal State,* pp. 169–170). Nevertheless, it was passed in an atmosphere of urgency and with little public debate.

Appendix: Worldwide Terrorism Since the World War II Period

BERNARD SCHECHTERMAN

State or Area	Terrorism by the State		Terrorism Directed Against the State	
	Targets Within the State	Targets Outside the State	Outside Supporter of Terrorism (State Supported Terrorism)[a]	Domestic Revolutionary Terrorist Organization[a]
Afghanistan	Muslim rebels, tribal groups			
Algeria			Ahl al-Dawah/Al-Qiyam (People of the Call, Muslim Brethren)—Egypt, Tunisia, Morocco; Jamaat al-Islamiyyah (Islamic Society)—Muslim Brethren, Egypt National Liberation Front (FLN)—Egypt	Ahl al-Dawah/Al-Qiyam (People of the Call, Muslim Brethren); Jamaat al-Islamiyyah (Muslim Brethren); National Liberation Front (FLN)
Argentina	Communists, the left		Ejercito Revolucionario del Pueblo (ERP)—Cuba, Trotskyites, USSR, Revolutionary Coordination Junta	Ejercito Revolucionario del Pueblo (ERP), Monteneros, Tacuara, Fuerzas Armados, Rebeldes (FAR), Movimento Argentino Nacional Organisacion (MANO), Argentine Anticommunist Alliance (AAA)
Bahrain			Jabhat al-Islamiyyah Lil-Tahrir al-Bahrain (Islamic Front for Liberation of Bahrain)—Iran, Iraq, Gulf States	Jabhat al-Islamiyyah Lil-Tahrir al-Bahrain (Shi'a)
Belgium			Fighting Communist Cells (CCC)—Direct Action	Fighting Communist Cells (CCC), Viaamse Militante Orden
Bolivia			Ejercito de Liberacion National (ELN)—Colombia, Peru ELN's, ERP	Ejercito de Liberacion National (ELN)
Brazil			M-19—Cuba, Nicaragua	Acao Liberidora Nacional (ALN), MR-8, Vanguardia Popular Revolucionaria (VPR), Vanguardia Armada Revolucionaria Palmares (VAR)
Bulgaria	Muslims	Italy		
Burma				Shan State Army
Cambodia	peasants (under Khmer Rouge)			
Canada				Front de Liberation du Quebec (FLQ)
Central African Republic	Tribal groups and individuals			
Chile	Communists, Socialists, the left		Movimento de Liberacion Nacional (MLN)—Tupamaros, Movimiento de la Izquierda Revolucionaria (MIR)—Peru, Venezuela MIR's, Manuel Rodrigues Patriotic Front—Libya	Movimento de Liberacion Nacional (MLN), Movimiento de la Izquierda Revolucionaria (MIR), Manuel Rodrigues Patriotic Front

	Terrorism by the State		Terrorism Directed Against the State	
State or Area	Targets Within the State	Targets Outside the State	Outside Supporter of Terrorism (State Supported Terrorism)[a]	Domestic Revolutionary Terrorist Organization[a]
Colombia			M-19—Cuba, Nicaragua; Ejercito de Liberacion Nacional (ELN)—Peru, Bolivia ELN's, Cuba; Fuerzas Armadas Revolucionarias de Colombia (FARC)—USSR	M-19, Ejercito de Liberacion Nacional (ELN), Ejercito Popular de Liberacion (EPL), Fuerzas Armadas Revolucionarias de Colombia (FARC), Quintin Lame (Indian)
Cuba	Batista elements and dissidents	Nicaragua, Dominican Republic, Colombia, Venezuela, Angola, Mozambique, Grenada		
Cyprus			Ethniki Organosis Kypriakou Agoniston (EOKA)—Greece	Ethniki Organosis, Kypriakou Agoniston (EOKA)
Czechoslovakia			Libya, Palestine Liberation Organization	
Dominican Republic			Macheteros—Cuba	Macheteros Partido Revolucionario Dominican (PRD)
East Germany		West Germany Ethiopia		
Ecuador				Alfaro Vive, Carajo
Egypt (There are between 50–60 opposition groups, but only some use terrorism)		Israel (Gaza Strip), Lebanon	Hizb Allah (Party of God)—N. Yemen; Hizb al-Tahrir (Liberation Party)—Arab countries; Ikhwan al-Muslimim (Muslim Brethren)—Gulf States, Syria, Jordan, Maghrib, Europe, Saudi Arabia; Jamaat al-Harakiyyah (Society of Action)—Libya; Jamaat al-Islamiyyah (Islamic Society)—Saudi Arabia; Jamaat al-Shariyyah (Society of Islamic Law)—Gulf States; Jamaat al-Tabligh (Society of Transmission)—Gulf States; Munazzamat al-Tahrir al-Islami (Islamic Liberation Organizational/ Technical Military Academy Group)—Syria, Sudan, Jordan, West Bank; Takfir wal-Hijrah (Denouncement and Holy Flight or Society of Muslims)—Kuwait, Gulf States, Turkey, Jordan, Libya, Pakistan, Syria, Saudi Arabia	Hizb Allah (Sunni), Hizb al-Tahrir (Sunni), Ikhwan al-Muslimim (Muslim Brethren), Jamaat al-Ahram (Pyramid Society), Jamaat al-Fath (Society of Conquest), Jamaat al-Haq (Society of Truth), Jamaat al-Harakiyyah (Society of Action), Jamaat al-Islamiyyah (Islamic Society), Jamaat al-Shariyyah (Muslim Brethren), Jamaat al-Tabligh, Jamaat al-Khalifah (Caliph's Group), Jamaat al-Muslimin lil-Takfir (Society for Accusation of Disbelief), Jamaat al-Muslimin (Muslim Group), Jamaat al-Takfir (Society of Denouncement), Al-Jihad (Holy War), Junud Allah (Soldiers of God), Junud al-Rahman (Soldiers of the Compassionate), Mukaffaratiyyah (Denouncers of Infidels), Munazzamat al-Tahrir al-Islami (Islamic Organizational/Technical Military Academy Group), Munazzamat al-Jihad (Jihad Organization), Qif wa Tabayyin (Halt & Prove), Qutbiyyin (Followers of Qutb), Samawiyyah (The Heavenly), Shabab Muhammad (Youth of Muhammad), Takfir wal-Hijrah (Denouncement and Holy Flight), Usbah al-Hashimiyyah (The Hashemite League)

State or Area	Terrorism by the State		Terrorism Directed Against the State	
	Targets Within the State	Targets Outside the State	Outside Supporter of Terrorism (State Supported Terrorism)[a]	Domestic Revolutionary Terrorist Organization[a]
Ethiopia	Urban Leninists, Menarchists, Tribal Groups, and Individual Dissidents	Sudan		Ethiopian People's Revolutionary Party (EPRP)
France			Direct Action—Fighting Communist Cells (Belgium), Corsican Front—Libya Breton Liberation Front/Breton Liberation Army (FLB-ARB)—Spanish ETA, Irish IRA	Direct Action, Corsican Front, Breton Liberation Front/Army
(West) German Republic			Baader-Meinhof or Red Army Faction (RAF)—PLO, Western European Marxist and Anarchist Groups; Revolutionare Zellen—Marxist and Anarchist Groups, Hoffman Military Sports Group—PLO	Baader-Meinhof or Red Army Faction, Bewegung 2. Juni, German Action Groups (Neo-Nazis), Revolutionare Zellen, Hoffman Military Sports Group
Great Britain			Provisional Irish Republican Army (PIRA)—Ireland and No. Ireland, Irish National Liberation Army (INLA)—Ireland and N. Ireland, Palestine Liberation Organization—Fatah, rejectionist factions, Iran-Iraqi officials, dissidents, Libyan dissidents	Provisional Irish Republican Army (PIRA), Irish National Liberation Army, Angry Brigade, Cadwyr Cymru (Keepers of Wales), Mudiad Amddiffyn Cymru (Movement for Defense of Wales)
Greece			International Solidarity/Christos Kassimis—Anarchists in West Europe	International Solidarity/Christos Kassimis, November 17 Movement
Guatemala	Indian Tribal Groups		Movimiento de Liberacion Nacional (MLN)—Tupamaros	Movimiento de Liberacion National (MLN), Fuerzas Armados Rebeldes (FAR), Mano Blanco (MANO), MR-13, Nueva Organisacion Anticommunista (NOA)
Gulf States			Ansar al-Dawah (Supporters of the Call)—Pakistan, India, Gulf States	Ansar al-Dawah (Supporters of the Call)
Haiti	Christian Sects and Individual Dissenters			
Holland			South Moluccans—Ambonese Indonesians	South Moluccans (Ambonese Indonesians)
India			Naxalites—Red China	Naxalites Sikhs
Indonesia	Timor Tribes			South Moluccans (Ambonese Indonesians)
Iran	Bahai, Jews, Mujahadeen, Shah supporters, Dissidents, Tudeh Communists, Kurds	Great Britain, Iraq, Saudi Arabia, Lebanon, Kuwait, Gulf States, France	Siakhal—Iraq, Libya, PLO; Kurdish Democratic Party (KDP)—USSR	Siakhal, Mujahadeen, Kurdish Democratic Party (KDP)

	Terrorism by the State		Terrorism Directed Against the State	
State or Area	Targets Within the State	Targets Outside the State	Outside Supporter of Terrorism (State Supported Terrorism)[a]	Domestic Revolutionary Terrorist Organization[a]
Iraq	Kurds, Shi'a, Communist Party, Tribal Groups, Islamic Groups	Iran, Syria, Lebanon, Kuwait, Bahrain, Saudi Arabia	Hizb al-Dawah al-Islamiyyah (Islamic Propagation Party)—Iran, Gulf States, Kuwait, Dubai, Lebanon, Bahrain; Rabitat al-Mara al-Muslimah (Muslim Women's Assn.)—Iran, Gulf States; Hizb al-Fatimi (The Fatima Party)—Iran, pro-Shah elements; Zaynab (Women's Assn.)—Iran; Hizb al-Thawri al-Islami (Islamic Revolutionary Party)—Iran; Ikhwan Muslimin (Muslim Brethren)— Egypt, Syria, Jordan, Saudi Arabia; Ijtihad al-Islami li-Talabat al-Iraqi (Islamic Iraqi Students Union)— Iran, Gulf States, USA, West Europe; Jamaat al-Ulama (Society of Ulama)—Iran; Majlis al-Thawra al-Islamiyyah (Islamic Revolutionary Council)—Iran; Mujahadeen (Fighters)—Iran; Munazzamat al-Amal al-Islami (Islamic Action Organization)—Iran; Rabitat al-Islamiyyah (Islamic Assn.)—Iran	Hizb al-Dawah al-Islamiyyah (Islam Propagation Party), Zaynab (Women's Assn.) Rabitat al-Mara al-Muslimah (Muslim Women's Assn.) Rabitat al-Islamiyyah (Islamic Assn.), Hizb al-Fatimi (the Fatima Party); Hizb al-Thawri al-Islami (Islamic Revolutionary Party), Ikhwan Muslimin (Muslim Brethren), Ittihad al-Islami li-Talabat al-Iraqi (Islamic Iraqi Students Union), Jamaat al-Ulama (Society of Ulama), Majlis al-Thawra al-Islamiyyah (Islamic Revolutionary Council), Mujahadeen (Fighters), Munazzamat al-Amal al-Islami (Islamic Action Organization), Kurdish Liberation Movement (Barzani)
Ireland, North			Provisional Irish Republican Army (PIRA)—Ireland, PLO, Libya, USA; Irish National Liberation Army (INLA)—Marxist Groups, Ireland	Provisional Irish Republican Army (PIRA), Irish National Liberation Army (INLA), Ulster Freedom Fighters (UFF), Ulster Volunteer Fighters (UVF), Ulster Defense Association (UDA), Protestant Action Force
Israel		Lebanon	Palestine Struggle Front (PSF)— PLO; Popular Front for Liberation of Palestine (PFLP)—Syria, PLO, Iraq; Al Fatah-Jordan, Syria, Iraq, Egypt, Libya, Algeria, Saudi Arabia	Stern Gang (Lehi), Irgun Zvi Leumi (Jabotinsky), Terrorists Against Terrorism (TNT)—West Bank, Ma'atz (Council of Young Delinquents), Palestine Struggle Front (PSF), Popular Front for Liberation of Palestine (PFLP), Al Fatah (Arafat), Usrah al-Jihad (Family of Jihad)
Italy			Red Brigades–Marxist/Anarchist Groups West Europe; League of Fighting Communists (LFC)— Marxist/Anarchist Groups West Europe	Red Brigades, Valpreda, Futurist Movement, League of Fighting Communists (LFC), Armed Proletarian Nuclei, NAR (Neo-Fascist), Ordine Nero (Neo-Fascist), MSI (Neo-Fascist)
Jordan	Al Fatah (PLO)	Israel, West Bank	Ansar Harakat Asna al-Quran (Supporters of the Sons of the Quran)—PLO; Harakat al-Tawhid (Movement of Unicity)—Anti-Arafat Palestinians, Iran; Hizb al-Tahrir al-Islami (Islamic Liberation Party)—Lebanon, Libya, Turkey, Palestinians; Al Fatah (Arafat)— Egypt, Syria, Iraq, Algeria, PLO, USSR, E. Europe	Ansar Harakat Asn al-Quran (Sons of The Quran), Harakat al-Tawhid (Movement of Unicity), Hizb al-Tahrir al-Islami (Islamic Liberation Party), Al Fatah (Arafat)
Korea (North)		South Korea		

124

	Terrorism by the State		Terrorism Directed Against the State	
State or Area	Targets Within the State	Targets Outside the State	Outside Supporter of Terrorism (State Supported Terrorism)[a]	Domestic Revolutionary Terrorist Organization[a]
Kuwait			Dar al-Tawhid (Unicity Publishers)—Iran, Iraq, Revolutionary Organization/Forces of the Prophet Muhammad—Lebanese Shi'a	Dar al-Tawhid (Unicity Publishers), Revolutionary Organization/Forces of the Prophet Muhammad
Laos			Pathet Laos—N. Vietnam	Pathet Laos
Lebanon[b]		Israel	AMAL (Hope)/Afwaj al-Muqawamah al-Lubnaniyyah (Lebanese Resistance Detachments)—Syria, Iran; Al-Jamaah al-Islamiyyah (Islamic Society, Muslim Brethren)—Syria, Jordan, Egypt; Jihad al-Islami (Islamic Holy War)—Syria, Iran; Hizb Allah/Islamic Amal (Party of God)—Iran, Syria; Arab Knights (Tripoli)—Arafat PLO; Saiqa (Vanguard)—Syria; Popular Front for Liberation of Palestine (PFLP)—Syria, Iraq, USSR; Popular Democratic Front for Liberation of Palestine (PDFLP)—Syria, Iraq, E. Europe, USSR; Al Fatah—USSR, Syria, Algeria, Iraq, So. Yemen, Egypt; Palestine Liberation Front (PLF)—Syria; Fatah Uprising (Abu Musa)—Syria; Fatah Revolutionary Council (Abu Nidal)—Syria, Iraq; Arab Liberation Front (ALF)—Iraq; Palestinian Popular Struggle Front (PPSF)—Syria; Popular Command (Jabril)—Syria; Palestine Liberation Front Breakaway (Muhammad Abbes); Lebanese Armed Revolution Faction (LARF)—Syria, PLO, Algeria; Lebanese Communist Party—Syria, USSR; National Syrian Social Party—Syria	AMAL (Hope); Al-Jamaah al-Islamiyyah (Islamic Society, Muslim Brethren); Jihad al-Islami (Holy War); Hizb Allah/Islamic AMAL (Party of God); Saiqa (Vanguard); Al Fatah (Arafat PLO); Lebanese Armed Revolution Faction (LARF); Arab Democratic Party; Nasserite Organizations (Sidon and Beirut); Lebanese Communist Party; National Syrian Social Party (NSSP); Arab Socialist Union
Libya	Dissidents among students, businessmen, and military	Egypt, Nicaragua, Great Britain, Sudan, Lebanon, Malta, USA, Greece, West Germany, Tunisia, Algeria, Philippines, Jordan, West Bank, France, Israel, Morocco, El Salvador, Guatemala, Pakistan, Portugal, New Caledonia, Thailand, Chile, Colombia, Turkey		Holy War

	Terrorism by the State		Terrorism Directed Against the State	
State or Area	Targets Within the State	Targets Outside the State	Outside Supporter of Terrorism (State Supported Terrorism)[a]	Domestic Revolutionary Terrorist Organization[a]
Mexico				Frente Urbano Zapatista (Zapata), Southern Liberation Army (ELS), Fuerzas Revolucionarias Armadas del Pueblo (FRAP)
Morocco			Ikhwan al-Muslimin/Shabibah al-Islamiyyah (Muslim Brethren)—Egypt, French Brethren	Ikhwan al-Muslimin (Muslim Brethren), Shubban Islamiyyah (Islamic Youth)
New Caledonia			Kanak Socialist National Liberation Front—Libya	Kanak Socialist National Liberation Front
Nicaragua	Miskito Indians	El Salvador, Honduras	Frente Sandinista de Liberacion Nacional (FSLN)—Cuba, USSR, Libya, East Europe; Contra Groups—USA, Honduras, Costa Rica; Miskito Indians	Frente Sandinista de Liberacion Nacional (FSLN); Contra Groups; Miskito Indians
Oman			Omani Liberation Front (OLF)—USSR, So. Yemen	Omani Liberation Front (OLF)
Peru			Ejercito de Liberacion Nacional (ELN)—ELN in Bolivia, Colombia; Movimiento de la Izquierda Revolucionaria (MIR)—MIR in Chile, Venezuela	Ejercito de Liberacion Nacional (ELN), Movimiento de la Izquierda Revolucionaria (MIR), Sendere Luminoso (Shining Path—Maoist), Tupac Amaru
Pakistan			Al-Zulfigar—Libya	Al-Zulfigar
Philippines			New People's Army—Libya, Saudi Arabia, Moro National Liberation Front—Libya	New People's Army, Moro National Liberation Front
Portugal			April 25 Movement (FP-25)—Libya	April 25 Movement (FP-25)
Puerto Rico			Macheteros—Cuba	Macheteros, Movimiento Independista Revolucionario Armado (MIRA), Commandos Armados de Liberacion (CAL), Fuerzas Armados de Liberacion Nacional (FALN)
El Salvador			Ejercito Revolucienario del Pueblo (ERP)—ERP Argentina, Farabundo Marti National Liberation Front (FMLN-5 groups)—Nicaragua, Cuba	Ejercito Revolucionario del Pueblo (ERP); Farabundo Marti National Liberation Front (FMLN)
Saudi Arabia			Hizb al-Tahrir al-Jazirah (Liberation Party of Jazirah)—Iran, Gulf States, Iraq, Bahrain; Al-Ikhwan (Muslim Brethren)—Egypt, Yemen, Pakistan, Gulf States; Jamaat al-Masjid (Mosque Society)—Gulf States, Oman; Munazzamat al-Thawrah al-Islamiyyah Shubuh fi al-Jazirah al-Aribiyyah (Islamic Revolutionary Organization in Arabian Peninsula)—Iran; Hejaz Liberation Front—Iraq	Hibz al-Tahrir al-Jazirah (Liberation Party of Jazirah), Al-Ikhwan (Muslim Brethren), Jamaat al-Masjid (Mosque Society), Munazzamat al-Thawrah al-Islamiyyah Shubuh fi al-Jazirah al-Arabiyyah (Islamic Revolutionary Organization in Arabian Peninsula), Hejaz Liberation Front
Senegal			Centre Social Islamique—Lebanon, Iran	Centre Social Islamique

| | Terrorism by the State | | Terrorism Directed Against the State | |
State or Area	Targets Within the State	Targets Outside the State	Outside Supporter of Terrorism (State Supported Terrorism)[a]	Domestic Revolutionary Terrorist Organization[a]
South Africa	African National Congress, Black dissenters, Black unions	Southwest Africa (Namibia)	African National Congress (ANC)—OAU, Black African States, USSR; Umkhonto we Sizwe (MK)—Cuba, Angola, E. Germany	African National Congress, Afrikaner Weer-standbewegung (AWB–Neo-Fascist), Umhkonto we Sizwe (MK), Azarian People's Organization (AZAPO)
Southwest Africa (Namibia)			Southwest Africa People's Organization (SWAPO)—Cuba, Angola	Southwest Africa People's Organization (SWAPO)
South Yemen (PDRY)		Oman, North Yemen, Lebanon		
Soviet Union (USSR)	Volga Germans, Tartars, Jews, Baltic Catholics, dissenters	Afghanistan, East European regimes, PLO (Arafat, rejectionist factions), some Communist parties in less developed countries		
Spain			Euzkadi ta Askatasanu (ETA V, VI)—Libya, PLO, French Basques; ETA VI-Liga Communista Revolucionari (LCR)—Anarchist/ Marxist groups; Warriors of Christ the King—Italian, South American Fascist Groups; Call of Jesus Christ—Lebanese Maronites	Euzkadi ta Askatasanu (ETA V, VI); ETA VI—Liga Communista Revolucionari (LCR); Frente Revolucionario Anti-Fascista y Patriota (FRAP); GAL; Anti-Terrorism ETA; Anti-Communist Apostolic Alliance (AAA); Spanish Basque Battalion (Neo-Fascist); New Force (Neo-Fascist)
Sri Lanka			Tamil Groups—India Tamils	Tamil Groups
Sudan			Sudanese People's Liberation Army/ Anya Nya II (SPLA)—Ethiopia, Libya	Sudanese People's Liberation Army/ Anya Nya II (SPLA)
Sweden			Kurdish Workers Party (KKK)—Kurds in Iran and Iraq; Croation Ustasha—Yugoslavia Croats	
Syria	Muslim Brethren groups	Lebanon, Israel, Jordan, Egypt, Iraq	Ikhwan al-Muslimin (Muslim Brethren)—Egypt, Iraq, Jordan, Gulf States; Ikhwan al-Muslimin (Political Solution Group)—Egypt, Gulf States, Iraq; Kataib Muhammad (Muslim Brethren of the Interior)—Egypt; Salafiyyah (Puritans)—Egypt; Tahririal-Islami (Islamic Liberation Party)—Jordan; Talia al-Muqatila lil Mujahadeen (Combat Vanguard of Fighters)—Iraq, Egypt	Ansari (Supporters); Ikhwan al-Muslimin (Muslim Brethren), Ikhwan al-Muslimin (Political Solution Group), Al-Jihad (Holy War), Junud Allah (Soldiers of God), Kataib al-Haq (Phalanges of Truth), Khulasah (Puritans), Salafiyyah (Puritans), Tahrir al-Islami (Islamic Liberation Party), Talia al-Muqatila lil Mujahadeen (Combat Vanguard of Fighters)
Tanzania	Zanzibar Arabs, Tribal resettlement (Ujamaa villages)	South Africa		
Thailand			Muslim Groups—Libya	

	Terrorism by the State		Terrorism Directed Against the State	
State or Area	Targets Within the State	Targets Outside the State	Outside Supporter of Terrorism (State Supported Terrorism)[a]	Domestic Revolutionary Terrorist Organization[a]
Tunisia			Amal al-Islami/Khawanjia (Islamic Action/Muslim Brethren)—Egypt; Hizb al-Islami (Islamic Party)—Egypt	Amal al-Islami/Khawanjia (Islamic Action), Progressive Socialist Gathering, Djihad Islamique, Ittijah al-Islami (Islamic Orientation), Jamiyyat Hifz al-Quran (Quran Preservation Societies), Hizb Allah al-Muktar, Parti de la Liberation Islamique (PLI) (Islamic Liberation Party), Movement for Popular Unity
Turkey	Kurds		Turkish People's Liberation Army (TPLA)—PLO, Syria, E. Germany, North Korea, USSR, Czechoslovakia; Armenian Secret Army (ASA)—USSR; ASALA (Armenian)—PLO, Libya, Syria, Greece	Nationalist Action Party, Turkish People's Liberation Army (TPLA), Armenian Secret Army (ASA), ASALA (Armenian), Kurdish Groups
Uganda	Tribes out of power			
United States			Aryan Nations—Neo-Nazis in Germany, Movimiento Independista Revolucionario Armado (MIRA)—Puerto Rico MIRA	Weathermen; Movimiento Independista Revolucionario Armado (MIRA); Symbionese Liberation Army (SLA); Aryan Nations; Covenant, Sword and Arm of the Lord (CSA); Posse Comitatus; The Order; White Aryan Resistance; White Patriot Party (WPP); National Alliance; Hanafi Muslims
Uruguay			Movimiento de Liberacion Nacional (Tupamaros)—Guatemala, Chile, Argentina Groups, USSR	Movimiento de Liberacion Nacional (Tupamaros)
Venezuela			Communist Party—Cuba, Movimiento de la Izquierda Revolucionaria (MIR)—Peru and Chile MIR's	Communist Party, Fuerzas Armados de Liberacion Nacional (FALN), Bandera Roja (Red Banner)
Vietnam (South and North)	South Vietnam officials (reeducation camps)	South Vietnam, Laos, Cambodia	Viet Cong—No. Vietnam	Viet Cong
Yemen (North)			Hizb Allah (Party of God)—Saudi Arabia, Gulf States	Hizb Allah (Party of God)
Yugoslavia			Croation Ustasha—USSR	Croation Ustasha
International			Muhammad Boudia Commando (Carlos)—Anarchist/Marxist Groups, PLO, Libya	
International[c]			Fatah (Arafat)—USSR, Arab League, Egypt, Libya, Syria, So. Yemen, Tunisia, Algeria, Lebanon, East Europe States, Jordan, Iraq, Iran, Sudan, Saudi Arabia, Kuwait, Gulf States; Arab Liberation Front (ALF)—Iraq; Palestine Liberation Front (PLF)—Iraq, Tunisia; Fatah Uprising (Abu Musa)—Syria; As Saiqa (Vanguard)—Syria; Palestine Front for Liberation of Palestine (PFLP) (Habash)—Syria, USSR;	

128

	Terrorism by the State		Terrorism Directed Against the State	
State or Area	Targets Within the State	Targets Outside the State	Outside Supporter of Terrorism (State Supported Terrorism)[a]	Domestic Revolutionary Terrorist Organization[a]
			Palestine Front for Liberation of Palestine, General Command (Jibril)—Syria; Palestine Struggle Front (PSF)—Syria; Palestine Liberation Front (PLF)—Syria; Democratic Front for Liberation of Palestine (DFLP) (Hawatmeh)—Syria, USSR; Fatah Revolutionary Council (Abu Nidal)—Syria, Libya; Palestine Liberation Front Breakaway—Syria; PALM—Syria; May 15th Movement—Syria; Palestine Front for Liberation of Palestine, Security Command—Syria; Palestine Front for Liberation of Palestine, General Command Breakaway—Syria.	

[a] It is not uncommon for a group to qualify under the heading of a domestic organization and also receive support from abroad. The domestic aspect indicates there is an indigenous basis for the origin and sustenance of the group apart from the overseas help.

[b] The Islamic Holy War and The Party of God operate by means of various subsidiary groups often brought into being for specific operations by members or by the leadership. Examples would be Organization of the Oppressed on Earth, Organization of Revolutionary Justice, etc. Many of the groups, particularly secular ones, are organized as part of the Lebanese National Democratic Front.

[c] The various Palestinian groups operate by means of various subsidiary groups often brought into being for specific operations by the leadership. Examples would be the Black September, Black June, Organization of Revolutionary Justice to Liberate Palestine, etc. The Palestinian groups most committed to "armed struggle" are also organized under the Palestine National Salvation Front. All are technically part of the larger organization popularly referred to and organized as the Palestine Liberation Organization.

The Contributors

William Lee Eubank, a graduate of the University of Oregon is an Assistant Professor of Political Science at the University of Nevada-Reno. He has authored or coauthored articles in voting theory, political contributions, computer and statistical methods and applications. Besides his current work on terrorism his interests are in political behavior, organizational behavior and applied statistics.

Joseph Richard Goldman is an assistant professor in the political science department at Minnesota. He is editor of *American Security in a Changing World: Issues and Choices* (1986), and has published articles in international relations and security policy. Professor Goldman has taught at the US Army Command & General Staff College in the areas of US national security, arms control, terrorism and counter insurgency, and is now working on several projects based on that year of teaching and research.

Michael M. Gunter is a professor of political science at Tennessee Technological University in Cookeville, Tennessee. He is the author of *"Pursuing the Just Cause of their People": A Study of Contemporary Armenian Terrorism* (Westport, Connecticut: Greenwood Press, 1986). Over the years he has published scholarly articles in such journals as the *American Journal of International Law, International Organization, Orbis,* and *Terrorism,* among numerous others. He also was a Senior Fulbright Lecturer in International Relations in Turkey.

Richard W. Leeman, a Ph.D. candidate at the University of Maryland, is currently an instructor of speech at Clemson University. He has research interests in terrorism, particularly regarding the Iranian hostage crisis, and has published on the oratory of Jimmy Carter.

Robert Maranto received a B.S. in Political Science at Maryland and is a Minnesotat ABD in the field. He is currently an Assistant Professor at the University of Southern Mississippi. He has presented papers exploring presidential power in comparative perspective and the political economy of guerrilla alliances. His chief research interests are the presidency, foreign policy and guerrilla warfare.

Edward P. Moxon-Brown was educated at the University of St. Andrews (Scotland); and the University of Pennsylvania (Philadelphia) where he was taught political science at the Queen's University of Belfast (Northern Ireland) where his main teaching and research interests include: West European integration, Irish politics, and political violence. Among his recent publications are: *Nation, Class and Creed in Northern Ireland* (1983), *Terrorism in France* (1983), 'Spain at the Threshold of the European Community' *Contemporary Review* (1983), 'Bridge and Chasma: Crosscutting Attitudes Among District Councillors in Northern Ireland' *Administration* (1984), 'The Water and the Fish: Public Opinion and the Provisional IRA in Northern Ireland *Terrorism: An International Journal* (1981).

Norman W. Provizer is an associate professor in the Department of History and Political Science at the Louisiana State University. He received his Ph.D. at the University of Pennsylvania. He is a former Research

Associate at the Foreign Policy Research Institute in Philadelphia. He is the editor of *Analyzing the Third World: Essays from Comparative Politics* (1978) and the author of articles that have appeared in Comparative Politics and the *Journal of African Studies*.

Gregory Rose is a member of the Department of Government faculty at the University of Texas. He has written extensively on Iran and, in particular, on the regime of the Ayatollah Khomeini. His more recent works include a contribution, *"Velayat-e Fagih and the Recovery of Islamic Identity in the Thought of Ayatollah Khomeini,"* in *Religion and Politics in Iran: Shi-ism from Quietism to Revolution* (Yale University Press, 1983).

Bernard Schechterman is a professor of politics at the University of Miami. He is the author of numerous articles on the politics of the Middle East. He is currently in the process of completing a manuscript on international relations in the Middle East.

Martin Slann is a professor of political science at Clemson University. He has authored an introductory text on comparative politics and a text for introductory political science classes.

Leonard Weinberg, Ph.D. Syracuse University (1967), is a professor of political science at the University of Nevada-Reno. He is the author of *After Mussolini: Italian Neo-Fascism and The Nature of Fascism* and co-author of *Comparing Public Policies*. In addition, Professor Weinberg's articles have appeared in *Terrorism,* the *Western Political Quarterly* and other journals. His current research interest is on terrorism and right-wing extremism in the industrial democracies. In 1984 Professor Weinberg was Fulbright Senior Research Fellow at the University of Florence.

Index

75, 76–77, 78–79
Morality, 7–9, 23
Motivation, 15–16, 17–18, 19; fad, 28–29; hatred, 24–26; irrational terrorism, 20–21; majority acceptance, 26–27; non-political power seeking, 27–28; personality fulfillment, 23–24
Munich massacre (1972), 34, 50
Muslims. *See* Islam
Mussavi, Husain, 27
Mussolini, Benito, 42

National Agricultural Bank of Piazza Fontana (Milan) bombing (1969), 81, 82
National Front (Italy), 82
National identity; Irish Catholics, 95, 96; Northern Ireland, 99–100
National Vanguard (Italy), 82
NATO. *See* North Atlantic Treaty Organization
Nayir, Sonner, 63
Nazis, 41, 44(nn 2, 3)
Negativism. *See* Adversary culture
Neo-Fascist groups, 115; Italy, 82–83, 84, 89, 90–91, 92, 93
New Ireland Forum, 100–101
New Order (Italy), 82
Nicaragua, 35, 41
Nidal, Abu, 34
Nixon administration, 50
Nonstate alliances, 13, 17
North Atlantic Treaty Organization (NATO), 12
Northern Ireland, 25, 36, 47, 51; alienation, 95–96, 97; antiterrorist strategies, 117–118, 119; British reactions, 106–108; Catholic community, 97–101; civil liberties, 117–118; judicial system, 101–104; national identity, 99–100; politics, 100–101, 104–106. *See also* Irish Republican Army
North-South Council of Ireland proposal, 107
Nuclear installations, 36, 37. *See also* Nuclear terrorism
Nuclear terrorism, 14, 34, 36–37

Occupational groups; Northern Ireland, 97–99; terrorist recruitment, 86(table), 88, 90

Olson, Mancur, 73, 74
Olympic massacre. *See* Munich massacre
Operation Phoenix, 35
Orly Airport bombing (1983), 57, 63, 66
Ouzounian, Levon, 58

Pacheco (president), 49
Paisley, Ian, 51
Palestine Front for the Liberation of Palestine, 26
Palestine Liberation Organization (PLO), 26, 34, 36
Palestinian Christians, 26
Palestinians, 24–25, 43, 51
Partisan Action Groups (Italy), 82
Pashabezian, Garabed, 59
Patriotism, 7–8
Peasants; Iranian revolution, 74–77; urbanization, 76–77, 79(nn 8, 14)
Personality fulfillment, 23–24
Peru, 36
Philanthropy, 28–29
PLO. *See* Palestine Liberation Organization
Police surveillance, 115
Policy, 33, 50
Political terrorism, 81–82, 84
Politics, 22, 95; affiliation, 87(table), 89; goals, 19, 20; Northern Ireland, 99–101, 104–107
Pol Pot regime, 41
Popkin, Samuel, 73, 74–75
Popular Front for the Liberation of Palestine, 49
Power seeking; nonpolitical, 27–28
Prejudice, 116
Prevention of Terrorism Act 1984 (PTA), 102
Primitivism, 42–43, 44(n5)
"Prisoners' Dilemma," 77–78
Private goods, 11
Profiteering, 15
Protestants; national identity, 99–100; Northern Ireland, 96, 98–99, 108
Provisional Sinn Fein (PSF), 101, 107; support, 104–106
PSF. *See* Provisional Sinn Fein
Psychology, 5, 35, 39; acceptance, 26–27; hatred, 24–26
PTA. *See* Prevention of Terrorism Act 1984

DATE DUE

MAR 02 2002	